Swedish Roots
The Legacy of George M. Stephenson
Pioneer and Patriot

Including an Introduction
by
H. Arnold Barton, Ph.D.
Southern Illinois University

Edited by
The Swedish Heritage Society
Publication Committee:

Ned Ratekin, Chair
Bob Lindell
Marilyn Boal
Norma Lindeen

2001

The Swedish Heritage Society
Swedesburg, Iowa

Published in Celebration of the
10th Anniversary
of the
Swedish American Museum
Swedesburg, Iowa

Copyright © 2001 by
THE SWEDISH HERITAGE SOCIETY
Swedesburg, Iowa
ISBN 0-9712430-0-X

Contents

Dedication v
Biographical Chart vii
Preface: From the Editors ix

INTRODUCTION
    H. Arnold Barton 1

A NOTE ON SWEDESBURG 7

WHEN AMERICA WAS THE LAND OF CANAAN
    George M. Stephenson 9

SOME FOOTNOTES TO THE HISTORY OF SWEDISH IMMIGRATION FROM ABOUT 1855 TO 1865
    George M. Stephenson 37

PILGRIM AND STRANGER
The Chronicles of George M. Stephenson
    I. America Fever 57
    II. A New Home in Swedesburg.............. 69
    III. A Boy's Life on the Family Farm........ 74
    IV. Learning At Home and School 86
    V. Social Life in Swedesburg.................. 98
    VI. The Move to the City.......................... 113
    VII. The Academy Years........................... 117
    VIII. Higher Education.............................. 128
    IX. Life as a Professor............................. 138
    X. Discovering Swedish Roots............... 142

Dedication

This volume is dedicated to George and Betty Stephenson whose pride in his father's achievements led them to initiate and sustain this project. Their support and generous sharing of information and materials have made this publication possible.

George and Betty Stephenson

George M. Stephenson, Jr., the elder son of George and Lilly Stephenson, accompanied them at age seven with his five year old brother Gordon to Sweden where his father carried out a full year of research under a Guggenheim Scholarship. During World War II Both George and Gordon were stationed in England serving in the Army Air Corp. George served as legal counsel to the M. and St. L. Railway from 1949 to 1954 and to the F.H. Peavey Grain Company from 1954 through 1962. He has been in private practice since 1962. He and his wife Elizabeth (Betty) have three children, Mark Stephenson, Peggy Rutman, and William Stephenson.

George M. Stephenson
1883-1958

George M. Stephenson
1883-1958

Family
Born Swedesburg, Iowa December 30, 1883
Eleventh child of Oliver and Mary Stephenson
Married Lilly Sundkvist January 14, 1918
George M. Stephenson Jr. born February 28, 1920
Gordon Arch Stephenson born November 30, 1921

Education
B. A. University of Chicago
A.B. Augustana College
Ph.D. Harvard University

Career Positions
Minnesota College
DePauw University
Dartmouth College
University of Minnesota

Appointments
Board of Education, United Lutheran Church
Board of Directors, Augustana College

Academic Fellowships
Guggenheim Fellowship, 1927
Fullbright Fellowship, 1954-1955

Honors and Awards
Decorated Knight of the North Star by King of Sweden
1937
Litt.D. Augustana College 1938
Ph.D. Honoris Causa Uppsala University 1938

Preface

George M. Stephenson broke new ground as an immigration historian by developing a distinctive method of presenting history. Rather than commenting and reflecting on events as a removed authority, he represented events through the words of those who lived them. He sifted through the letters, documents, decrees, and public statements of those who lived during the times under study to identify the dreams and motivations, the challenges and fears, the causes and effects that were related to history's events.

Applying this style in his studies of immigration, Stephenson discloses through the Swedish immigrants' own words what motivated them to leave home and nation for the unknown in America during the latter half of the 19th century. The first article in this volume, **When America Was the Land of Canaan,** holds this mirror to events during the great Swedish emigration.

In this style also he portrays how the persons remaining at home in Sweden, family, friends, officials of government and the church, responded personally and institutionally to the event that left gaping holes in families, communities, and in the conduct of business and government in Sweden. The second article in this volume, **Some Footnotes to the History of Swedish Immigration from about 1855 to about 1865**, captures such reactions.

The third article in this volume, **Pilgrim and Stranger**, presents Stephenson's own life as history. It is the product of his diaries; it is his memoirs; and it is a work he labored over for several years, yet never published. It appears here in published form for the first time, and we are grateful to George Stephenson, Jr. for providing us the manuscript. In this work Stephenson's objective style is clearly present, but he increasingly offers more personal judgment and conclusions concerning the state of education, politics, war, and most insightfully, the integration of immigrants into America's culture.

One fact readers of *Pilgrim and Stranger* must know: he was an avid fan of baseball. The Faculty Senate at the University of Minnesota adopted by a rising vote a resolution praising Stephenson at his death for "his thoroughgoing scholarship, his substantial contributions, his fearless candor, his sharp-tongued wit, and his skill as a storyteller." The resolution also stated, "Professor Stephenson's many interests included baseball, and his legion of friends hoped that some day he would write a history of this sport."

The Editorial Committee is grateful to **H. Arnold Barton** for so graciously providing the introduction to this volume, and to **Gregory M. Britton** and the Minnesota Historical Society Press for permission to reprint the Stephenson articles, and of course a special acknowledgement is due **George Stephenson Jr.** for stimulating and maintaining this project.

Through this publication the people of Swedesburg are pleased to honor a native son, George M. Stephenson, whose life's work in documenting the story of the great Swedish immigration has provided us with a deeper knowledge of our heritage.

Editorial Committee: Ned Ratekin, Chair
Bob Lindell
Marilyn Boal
Norma Lindeen

H. ARNOLD BARTON, Professor Emeritus at Southern Illinois University, is a former editor of the Swedish American Historical Quarterly. *He has received numerous awards for his work in immigration history, including the Swedish American Historical Society Carl Sandburg Medal, the Ellis Island Medal, and The Vasa Order of Sweden Swedish American of the Year Award. Most recently he was awarded the rank of Commander of the Royal Order of the Polar Star from King Carl XVI Gustaf of Sweden.*

INTRODUCTION

H. Arnold Barton
Southern Illinois University at Carbondale

Passing through Swedesburg, Iowa, some years ago, I took a stroll through the old cemetery by the Lutheran church, examining the old Swedish tombstones. At the back, near a cornfield, I saw a newer stone simply inscribed STEPHENSON. From the names, Mary and Oliver Stephenson, and their dates on the adjoining tombstone I realized that I had come upon the true pioneer not only of Swedish immigration history but of American immigration history as a whole: George Malcolm Stephenson.

His grandparents, Steffan and Christina Catharina Steffansson, emigrated from Sweden in 1849 with their eight children to Peter Cassel's New Sweden near Lockridge, Iowa, the earliest lasting Swedish settlement in the Middle West, established only four years before. Already in 1855, both parents and five of their children died of cholera. Their surviving son Oliver (Olaus) married Mary (Maria) Zackrisson, also from Sweden, and moved with other New Sweden settlers to richer farmlands around Swedesburg. Here George, the youngest of their eleven children, was born in 1883.

George Stephenson attended Augustana College in Rock Island, Illinois, and earned bachelor's degrees both there and at the University of Chicago. After teaching some years at Minnesota College in Minneapolis, he pursued a doctoral degree at Harvard. Here he studied with the celebrated historian of the American West, Frederick Jackson Turner, who emphasized the ways of life of common folk. Stephenson was attracted to immigration history for this very reason, but Turner persuaded him to write his dissertation on public lands policy.

From 1914 until he retired in 1952, Stephenson taught at the University of Minnesota. Here he soon turned to Swedish immigration history. In 1919 he brought out his first article in the field, on the Swedish Americans and World War I. This was followed in 1922 by "Some Footnotes to the History of Swedish Immigration from about 1855 to about 1865" and "Typical 'America Letters," the latter consisting of correspondence within his mother's family, and in 1923 his "*Hemlandet* Letters," culled from that Swedish-American newspaper in Chicago. In these articles Stephenson already reveals a lifelong inner conflict between attachment to his own heritage and the demands of critical scholarship.

Meanwhile, Stephenson was working on a book that would be a true landmark in American historical scholarship, *History of American Immigration, 1820-1924,* published in 1926. A good deal had previously been written about immigration, particularly since the 1890s, but it was the work of laymen contributing to public debate over immigration. Prominent Anglo-Americans had treated it as a "problem." Record high immigration around the turn of the century seemed to them a threat to America's fundamental values and way of life, and they urged that it be restricted. Such writings contributed to the rising tide of anti-foreign sentiment that resulted in the "100-percent" Americanism during World War I and the immigration quota laws of the 1920s. On the other side, immigrant historians, likewise laymen, strove to glorify their peoples, in both the Old World and the New, to bolster ethnic pride and gain respect in the wider American society. Among the Swedish Americans, the Chicago newspaper editor Johan A. Enander would be the prime example.

George Stephenson's book in 1926 ushered in a new era of immigration research by professional historians. Many, like Stephenson, were of Scandinavian background. Before this time, American historians had considered the subject of little interest.

Stephenson meanwhile continued to cultivate the history of the Swedes in America. In 1926 he brought out "An America Letter of 1849," written from New Sweden, Iowa, by his grandfather, Steffan Steffansson. Important contributions were "Documents Relating to Peter Cassel and the Settlement at New Sweden" in 1929 and *Letters Relating to Gustaf Unonius and the Early Swedish Settlers in Wisconsin* in 1937. His article "When America Was the Land of Canaan," which he later regarded as the best thing he had ever written, meanwhile appeared in 1929.

In publishing the private letters of ordinary immigrants Stephenson likewise proved himself a pioneer. Previously letters written for publication, together with autobiographical writings by prominent persons had appeared in print. For Stephenson immigration was above all the story of ordinary men and women, and their voices deserved to be heard.

Most of Stephenson's writings during the 1920s came out in the publications of the Swedish Historical Society of America, which he edited, from 1921 to 1929, publishing many original documents in both the original Swedish and in English translation. The society had been established in 1905 with J. A. Enander as its first president. Most of its members were amateurs who, in the Enander tradition, were bent upon glorifying and commemorating their countrymen in America. Stephenson strove valiantly to set higher standards of historical objectivity, as the Norwegian-American Historical Association, established in 1925, had managed to do under the guidance of his departmental colleague at Minnesota, Theodore Blegen.

In the end these efforts proved disillusioning. Stephenson later complained that the Swedish Americans were not interested in their history. In actuality, they were too strongly attached to the older tradition of self-glorification to find much appeal in his strict scholarly criteria. They now gave enthusiastic support to J. A. Enander's true disciple, Dr. Amandus Johnson, and his Swedish-American Historical Museum in Philadelphia, which opened in 1938, a veritable shrine to a glorious Swedish presence in America.

There was however another factor. In 1932 Stephenson published his *Religious Aspects of Swedish Immigration,* a work of lasting significance, which was in many respects critical of the Augustana Lutheran Synod, the largest Swedish-American religious denomination. The book aroused widespread indignation. By 1934 the Swedish Historical Society of America quietly went out of existence.

Henceforward Stephenson devoted himself to a biography of the Swedish American governor of Minnesota, John Lind, a maverick like himself, published in 1935, thereafter to a study of the Puritan heritage in America that came out in 1952. Although he received honors from the Swedish government, he professed to have no further interest in Swedish-American subjects and in 1948 advised against the founding of the Swedish Pioneer (now Swedish-American) Historical Society. Stephenson likewise felt that he was unjustly unappreciated by the American historical profession at large. He died in Minneapolis in 1958.

Only two years later, in 1960, a one-time student of his, the British historian Frank Thistlethwaite, issued a call at the International Congress of Historians in Stockholm for renewed study of the Great Migration. Since then, down to the present, it has been an intensely cultivated field, on both sides of the Atlantic, and beyond, not least by historians of the Swedes in America. Though he is all too little remembered today, his life work has been powerfully vindicated since his death.

It is a particular satisfaction for me to introduce this reissue of two of George Stephenson's more important articles. His grandfather and father emigrated from Södra Vi parish in northeastern Småland. This is my own ancestral Swedish parish and I am proud to be myself distantly related to this distinguished American historian.

*

Principal Publications by George M. Stephenson

The Political History of the Public Lands from 1840 to 1862. Boston, 1917.

"The Attitude of Swedish Americans toward the World War," *Proceedings of the Mississippi Valley Historical Association* 10 (1918-19): 79-94.

The Conservative Character of Martin Luther. Philadelphia, 1921.

"Typical America Letters," *Yearbook of the Swedish Historical Society of America, 1921-23,* 52-98.

"Some Footnotes to the History of Swedish Immigration from about 1855 to about 1865," *Yearbook of the Swedish Historical Society of America* 7 (1922): 33-52.

A History of American Immigration, 1820-1924. New York, 1926.

"The Background of the Beginning of Swedish Immigration, 1850-1875," *American Historical Review* 31 (1926): 708-31.

The Founding of the Augustana Synod. Rock Island, IL, 1927.

"When America Was the Land of Canaan," *Minnesota History* 10 (1929): 237-60.

"Documents Relating to Peter Cassel and the Settlement at New Sweden," (trans. and ed.), *Swedish American Historical Bulletin* 2:1 (1929), 1-82. Reprinted (minus the texts in Swedish) in H. Arnold Barton, ed., *Peter Cassel & Iowa's New Sweden* (Chicago, 1995), 67-114.

"The Mind of the Scandinavian Immigrant," *Norwegian-American Studies and Records,* 4 (Northfield, MN, 1929), 63-73.

The Religious Aspects of Swedish Immigration. Minneapolis, 1932.

Letters Relating to Gustaf Unonius and the Early Swedish Settlers in Wisconsin, (trans. and ed.). Augustana Historical Society Publications, 7 (Rock Island, IL, 1937).

John Lind of Minnesota. Minneapolis, MN 1935.

American History since 1865. New York, 1939.

American History to 1865. New York. 1940.

The Puritan Heritage. New York, 1952.

"Rip Van Winkle in Sweden," *Swedish Pioneer Historical Quarterly* 7 (1956): 47-60.
*

The fullest account of George Stephenson's life and career is Rudolph J. Vecoli's article, "'Over the years I have encountered the hazards and rewards that await the historian of immigration': George Malcolm Stephenson and the Swedish-American Community," *Swedish-American Historical Quarterly* 51 (2000): 130-49.

A Note on Swedesburg

In George Stephenson's memoirs, *Pilgrim and Stranger*, he says, "I think of [Swedesburg] as a home from which I have never been absent." Although he spent only ten childhood years in Swedesburg, he received there a sense of community that never left him. He speculates that outward appearances may have led visitors to consider Swedesburg "drab and uninteresting." "But," he says, "my own experiences and observations testify to the contrary. There was virtue in hard work. Self-respect inspired wholesome rivalry to raise fine crops, to build comfortable homes, to improve farms, and to win the confidence of neighbors." Swedesburg was a concept as well as a place to Stephenson, as it is to many of its residents today.

As a child living in rural Swedesburg George did not see an electric light or visit a city until he was ten years old; but he saw his parents welcome new immigrants from the homeland, provide them with food, clothing, and housing if necessary, and help them get started on their own success. From these experiences in Swedesburg with a community of immigrant families he eventually became a distinguished scholar in the field of immigration history.

Swedesburg today appears as a small area with a few plotted streets, but that view limits the truth of Swedesburg. Swedesburg is a community of a few businesses, a village of approximately 100 residents, a countryside of two dozen farms extending over 7000 acres, and an increasing number of descendants who left the area but not the spirit of the community.

When originally settled, much of the region was marshland. A surveyor in 1868 noted on the margin of his papers, "It will in all probability never be settled, but nevertheless, there are a few Swedes moving in." Settlers arriving at the nearby county seat of Mount Pleasant were told that no one is moving out there, except a few Swedes.

Those Swedes were creating ditches and then tiling the land to carry off the water. Over time more and more land was reclaimed, and fertile, prosperous farms now cover the area. Those Swedes built schools and earnestly guided their children in becoming American. They founded a church, of which Oliver Stephenson, George's father, was a charter member, serving as a deacon, a trustee, and a leader of the congregation.

Those Swedes were persistent in their faith. The first church was lost to fire. Their new church, a landmark because of its tall steeple, was struck by lightening and burned to the ground. A third church, built of brick, now stands sturdily on the same historic site serving the several hundred members of its congregation.

The Swedish language disappeared over time, even in the church, as the community adjusted to American ways. But the Swedish customs were slower to die, and when even those began to disappear with the passing of the generations, the descendants resolved to preserve and share their heritage for future generations. In 1986 they formed the Swedish Heritage Society, and in 1991 opened the Swedish American Museum, an increasingly successful heritage destination.

Each year the Society sponsors the traditional Swedish celebrations of Midsommer and St. Lucia Day. Also, the Swedesburg Evangelical Lutheran Church holds a Christmas season *Smorgasbord* attended by hundreds from around the region. Swedesburg still survives today, a tidy village of 40 homes, a landscape of productive farms, and a thriving sense of purpose in preserving its heritage.

This article was included in "Selections from 'Minnesota History', A Fiftieth Anniversary Anthology," pp. 138-155 (1929). *Minnesota Historical Quarterly.* Eds. Rhoda R. Gilman and June Drenning Holmquist. Reprinted by permission.

When America Was the Land of Canaan

GEORGE M. STEPHENSON

VOLUMES HAVE BEEN WRITTEN on the causes of emigration from the various countries of Europe to the United States, and it may appear superfluous to add to the numerous articles that have appeared in print.[1] A plethora of emigration statistics is available; monographs have appeared by the score; and it would seem that the subject has been attacked from every conceivable angle. But the historical profession still awaits the man with the magic touch, who by a process known only to the master can convert this tremendous mass of material into a masterpiece of historical synthesis. This master must sound the depths of the human soul, and he must analyze the noblest as well as the basest emotions that play on the human heart. He will not concern himself with the people on whom fortune has smiled graciously, nor will he relate the exploits of the battlefield and portray the lives of kings and nobles; he will study the documents that betray the spirit, hopes, and aspirations of the humble folk who tilled the soil, felled the forest, and tended the loom — in short, who followed the occupations that fall to the lot of the less favored majority that exists in every land.

Emigration from Sweden was a class movement that spread from the rural districts to the cities and towns. The fever sought its victims among those who were not inoculated with the virus of social distinction and economic prosperity; and when the epidemic was transported three thousand miles across the water, it took a more virulent form. In fact, it was transmitted most effectively by the thousands of letters that found their way from America to the small red cottages hidden among the pine-clad, rocky hills of Sweden.

It has become a commonplace that emigration from Sweden began in earnest after the close of the American Civil War, when, according to a newspaper account published in 1869, "the emigrants, as if by agreement, gathered from the various communities on certain days, like migratory swallows, to leave, without apparent regret, the homes and associations of their native land, in order to begin a new life on another continent."[2] Statistically this statement is accurate enough, but historically it is entirely misleading. Emigration from Sweden began in earnest in the decade of the 1 840s, when the first "America letters" found their way back to the old country. These letters made a tremendous impression on certain persons at a time when a new world —a new and ideal world — was dawning in literature and in the press.[3] Into this realm of the idealist the "America letters" fell like leaves from the land of Canaan. They were not only read and pondered by the simple and credulous individuals to whom they were addressed, and discussed in larger groups in homes and at markets and fairs and in crowds assembled at parish churches, but they were also broadcast through the newspapers, which, unwittingly or not, infected parish after parish with the

"America fever." The contents of these documents from another world were so thrilling and fabulous that many editors were as glad to publish them as were the recipients to have them published. The result was that the most fanciful stories were circulated about the wonderful country across the Atlantic — a land of milk and honey.

A correspondent from Linköping wrote to a Jönkoping paper in May, 1846, as follows: "The desire to emigrate to America in the country around Kisa is increasing and is said to have spread to neighboring communities. A beggar girl from Kisa, who has gone up into the more level country to ply her trade, is said to have painted America in far more attractive colors than Joshua's returned spies portrayed the promised land to the children of Israel. 'In America,' the girl is reported to have said, 'the hogs eat their fill of raisins and dates that everywhere grow wild, and when they are thirsty, they drink from ditches flowing with wine.' Naturally the gullible *bondfolk* draw the conclusion from such stories that it is far better to be a hog in America than to be a human being in Sweden. The emigration fever seizes upon them, and the officials are so busy making out emigration permits that they cannot even get a night's rest."[4]

One cannot escape the suspicion that this beggar girl from Kisa had read or had heard discussed a letter written at Jefferson County, Iowa, on February 9, 1846, by Peter Cassel, who the previous year had led a party of twenty-one emigrants — men, women, and children — from this parish. The departure of this man in his fifty-sixth year at the head of a large company of emigrants — large for that time — created a sensation in his parish and in neighboring parishes; and information about his adventure was eagerly awaited by his large circle of friends and relatives. And they were not disappointed. In describing the wonders of America, Cassel's pen vied with Marco Polo's. Iowa's corn, pumpkins, and hogs, seen through the medium of his letters, appeared as monstrous to the peasants of Sweden as Gulliver to the inhabitants of Lilliput; and in contrast with the earnings of the American farmer the income of the Swedish husbandman shrank to insignificance. Even the thunder in Sweden sounded like the report of a toy pistol, compared with the heavy artillery of the heavens in America.[5]

In his first letter Cassel wrote thus: "The ease of making a living here and the increasing prosperity of the farmers . . . exceeds anything we anticipated. If only half of the work expended on the soil in the fatherland were utilized here, the yield would reach the wildest imagination. . . . Barns and cattle sheds are seldom, if ever, seen in this vicinity; livestock is allowed to roam the year around, and since pasturage is common property, extending from one end of the land to the other, a person can own as much livestock as he desires or can take care of, without the least trouble or expense. . . . One of our neighbors . . . has one hundred head of hogs. . . . Their food consists largely of acorns, a product that is so abundant that as late as February the ground is covered in places. . . . Corn fields are more like woods than grain fields."

This *bonde* (landowning farmer) not only was impressed with America's rich soil, its forests, its abundance of coal and metals, its rivers and lakes swarming with fish, but also wanted his friends at home to know that in other respects he had found a better world: "Freedom and equality are the fundamental principles of the constitution of the United States. There is no such thing as class distinction here, no counts, barons, lords or lordly estates....[6] Everyone lives in the unrestricted enjoyment of personal liberty. A Swedish *bonde,* raised under oppression and accustomed to poverty and want, here finds himself elevated to a new world, as it were, where all his former hazy ideas of a society conforming more closely to nature's laws are suddenly made real and he enjoys a satisfaction in life that he has never before experienced. There are no beggars here and there never can be so long as the people are ruled by the spirit that prevails now. I have yet to see a lock on a door in this neighborhood. . . . I have never heard of theft. . . . At this time of the year the sap of the sugar maple is running and we have made much sugar and syrup."[7]

If the beggar girl from Kisa had heard this letter read and discussed by simple-minded folk, little wonder that her imagination ran away with her. Surely Joshua's spies could not have found a more ideal land if they had gone to the ends of the earth. And this girl was not the only purveyor of "information" about America. In many parishes stories were current that in Gothenburg there was a bureau that provided emigrants with all the necessities for the journey — free of charge; that several vessels were waiting to transport emigrants to the promised land — also free of charge; that in two days enough money could be earned to buy a cow that gave fabulous quantities of milk; that all pastures were common property; that the grass grew so tall that only the horns of the grazing cattle were visible; that there were no taxes in that fortunate land; that rivers ran with syrup; that cows roamed at large and could be milked by anyone.[8]

There may have been occasional "America letters" published in the newspapers of Sweden prior to 1840, but they were rare, chiefly because the few Swedes in America were usually adventurers or deserters from vessels, who did not find it expedient to let their whereabouts be known. The interest of the press in these letters began with the publication in *Aftonbladet,* in January, 1842, of a long letter from Gustaf Unonius, a young man who had received some notice as the author of a volume of poems before emigrating with his bride and a few of the "better folk" in the early autumn of 1841. He used the columns of this widely read Stockholm daily to inform his friends and acquaintances, especially in and around Upsala where he had been a student, about his experiences in the new world.

Unonius was essentially a student and his letters were carefully phrased, with the advantages and disadvantages of America weighed in the balance; but he could write after a residence of one month in Wisconsin that it was unlikely that he would ever return to his native land, because he found his youthful dream of a republican form of government and a democratic society realized. He found no epithets of degradation applied to men of humble toil; only those whose conduct merited it were looked down upon. "Liberty still is stronger in my affections than the bright silver dollar that bears her image," he wrote. Three months later he could write: "I look to the future with assurance. The soil that gives me sustenance has become my home; and the land that has opened opportunities and has given me a home and feeling of security has become my new fatherland." The readers of his letters learned that the young idealist, seeking to escape from the trammels of an older society, had found something that approached a Utopia on the American frontier, although his writings about it resembled more the reflections of a man chastened by unaccustomed toil and hardships than the song of a pilgrim who had crossed the river Jordan.[9]

Within a few weeks an emigrant who preceded Unonius to Wisconsin by three years was heard from through the same journalistic medium, the man to whom the letters were addressed having been prompted to publish them by reading the Unonius document. The writer was John Friman, a member of a party consisting of a father and three sons, who settled at Salem, Wisconsin Territory, in 1838. The serious illness of the youngest son necessitated the return to Sweden of father and son, but the eldest son remained to carry on the correspondence with the "folks back home."[10]

14

In a later letter the young pioneer told about his first meeting with Unonius in the latter's home at New Upsala: "We are healthier and more vigorous than we ever were in Sweden. Many people from England and Ireland have already come here. Last fall, in October, a few Swedes from Upsala came here from Milwaukee, Mr. Gustaf Unonius and wife, married only six weeks when they left Sweden. A relative, Inspector Groth, and a Doctor Pålman have settled on a beautiful lake near a projected canal, twenty-eight miles west of Milwaukee, Milwaukee County. They have named the settlement New Upsala *and the capital of New Sweden in Wisconsin.* They are expecting several families and students from Upsala this summer. . . . I visited New Upsala last fall. They wanted me to sell out and move there. Father has probably heard of them. Last fall Unonius wrote to *Aftonbladet.* I hope his letter will awaken the desire to emigrate among the Swedes. . . .Altogether we own two hundred acres of land, and when we have our farm fenced and eighty acres broken . . . I wouldn't trade it for a whole estate in Sweden, with all its ceremonies. Out here in the woods we know nothing of such. . . . Give our love to Herman and say to him that we hope his health will be better than it was the first time he was here."[11]

Herman's health was restored sufficiently to enable him, in company with a young man from another city, to undertake the journey to the "states" a few weeks later. Imagine the sorrow of the father when he received a letter informing him that Herman had entirely disappeared, his companion, who had arrived at the Friman farm in due time, being unable to give a satisfactory explanation of the mystery.[12] The public in Sweden was informed of the misfortune through the publication of the letter in the papers, and interest was even more quickened by the letter from the father of the companion, answering *seriatim* the charges of the elder Friman brother that Herman was the victim of misplaced confidence in his fellow traveler;[13] for weeks thousands eagerly searched the columns of the papers for the latest word about "brother Herman." The wonderful adventures the prodigal son related when he finally accounted for himself at the Friman farm not only cleared the name of his companion and relieved the anxiety of both fathers, but it gave to the "America letters" a halo of romance that made them, in a very real sense, news letters from the rich, mighty, and romantic land out there in the West.[14] The muse of history suffers no violence by the assertion that one of the most interesting and widely read features of the Swedish papers were the "America letters."

In that unique and valuable work that emerged from the survey of a commission appointed by the Swedish government to seek out the causes of emigration, appeared a volume entitled "The Emigrants' Own Reasons," comprising letters written at the request of the commission by Swedish immigrants who had lived a longer or shorter period in the United States and Canada.[15] These letters have their value, but it must be recognized that the writers unconsciously injected into them the retrospections of several months or years. There is, therefore, a vast difference between these letters and the "America letters" — naïve accounts of experiences written for relatives and friends, who were as simple and naïve as the writers themselves, and before retrospection had wrought its havoc. It is just this "unconscious" and naïve quality of the "America letters" that opens for the historian windows through which he can look into the cottages in Sweden and into the log cabins in the adopted country. The student of emigration who is satisfied with poring over statistics, government reports, and "social surveys" will never sound the depths of one of the most human phenomena in history. The much-abused psychologist in this instance is an indispensable colaborer with the historian, for the theme of the historian of emigration is the human soul. The emigrant was a product of his environment, but he was not held in bondage by it; his soul could not be shackled, even though his body was the slave of harsh taskmasters.

In the large the contents of the "America letters" written in the years from 1840 to 1860 may be divided into two categories: (1) impressions of and experiences in America; and (2) comments on conditions in Sweden. With the exception of a few letters written by men of the type of Gustaf Unonius, the great mass of them were the products of men who had only a meager education and who grew to manhood before the generation that enjoyed the advantages provided under the act of 1842, by which every parish was required to provide a public school. The spelling is faulty, to say the least, and the punctuation is atrocious. New York becomes "Nefyork" and "Nevyork"; Chicago, "Sikago" and "Cicaga"; Illinois, "Elinojs"; Iowa, "Adiova" and "Jova"; Pennsylvania, "Pensarvenien"; Galesburg, "Gillsborg" and "Galesbury"; Albany, "Albano" and "Albanes"; Troy, "Troij"; Princeton, "Princeldin"; Rock Island, "Rockislan" and "Rackarlan"; Peru, "Pebra" and "Perru"; and Henry County, "Hendi counti." Not only were liberties taken with American place names but even many innocent Swedish words were mutilated beyond recognition.

But the person who has the patience to spell his way through a mass of these documents cannot fail to acquire a profound respect for the ability of the writers to express themselves and for their sound and wholesome instincts. They reveal that in their native land they had thought seriously, and even deeply, about their own problems and those of their communities — probably more than they or their neighbors at the time realized; but it was during the first weeks and months in America that they gave vent to their feelings and emotions and tried the powers of expression that had previously lain dormant. America gave them a basis for comparison and contrast: church, government, society, and officials at home appeared in an entirely different light; and the contrast was such that the emigrant had no desire to return in order to relate to his countrymen his strange experiences; on the contrary, he did all in his power to urge them to follow his example — to emigrate. The emigrant became an evangelist, preaching the gospel of America to the heavy-laden. For him the year of jubilee had come.

There are, of course, among the "America letters" that have been preserved a number that express regret that the transatlantic adventure was undertaken and reveal a feeling of bitterness towards those who had painted America in such attractive colors and in that way had lured the writers into poverty and misery; but the overwhelming number of them are almost ecstatic in praise of the adopted country and bitterly hostile to the land that gave them birth. Some writers even went to the length of ridiculing or deriding those to whom their letters were addressed for remaining in a land unworthy of the man and woman of honest toil and legitimate ambition.

Extracts from two letters written before 1850 are illuminating in this regard: "I doubt that any one will take the notion of returning to Sweden, because the journey is too long and expensive; and even if these considerations were minor with certain individuals, I doubt that they would go, for the reason that nothing would be gained. . . . Not until this year have I fully realized how grateful we ought to be to God, who by His grace has brought us away from both spiritual and material misery. How shall we show our appreciation for all the goodness the Lord has bestowed upon us! In like manner does He bid you, my relatives and friends, to receive the same grace and goodness, but you will not heed His voice. What will the Lord render unto you now? He will allow you to be deprived of all this during your entire lives and in the future to repent bitterly of your negligence. We have the word of prophecy . . . and you will do well to heed it. . . . Ought not a place of refuge and solace be acceptable to you? . . . Now

I have said what my conscience prompts me to say and on you rests the responsibility for yourselves and your children."[16]

The other letter contains the following admonition: "Tell Johannes and others not to condemn me for failing to return home at the appointed time, as I promised and intended when I left Sweden, because at that time I was as ignorant as the other stay-at-homes about what a voyage to a foreign land entails. When a person is abroad in the world, there may be many changes in health and disposition, but if God grants me health I will come when it pleases me. If it were not for the sake of my good mother and my relatives, I would never return to Sweden. No one need worry about my circumstances in America, because I am living on God's noble and free soil, neither am I a slave under others. On the contrary, I am my own master, like the other creatures of God. I have now been on American soil for two and a half years and I have not been compelled to pay a penny for the privilege of living. Neither is my cap worn out from lifting it in the presence of gentlemen. There is no class distinction here between high and low, rich and poor, no make-believe, no 'title sickness,' or artificial ceremonies, but everything is quiet and peaceful and everybody lives in peace and prosperity. Nobody goes from door to door begging crumbs. . . .The Americans do not have to scrape their effects together and sell them in order to pay heavy taxes to the crown and to pay the salaries of officials. There are no large estates, whose owners can take the last sheaf from their dependents and then turn them out to beg. Neither is a drink of *brännvin* forced on the workingman in return for a day's work. . . . I sincerely hope that nobody in Sweden will foolishly dissuade anyone from coming to this land of Canaan."[17]

This letter may be said to be a prototype of the "America letters." It contains a mass of details, and almost every sentence breathes a deep-seated dissatisfaction with government, institutions, and society in Sweden and at the same time a remarkable satisfaction with everything American. This tone is characteristic even of letters written by persons whose first experiences in the new country were anything but pleasant. A man from Småland, who emigrated with his wife and eight children in 1849 — one of the "cholera years" — buried one of his daughters on the banks of an inland canal, suffered several weeks with malaria, and just escaped being cheated out of his hard-earned savings, was happy over his decision to emigrate and looked to the future with high hopes for a better existence in spiritual as well as material matters.[18] Another enthusiast, who had been exposed to dangers of various kinds, wrote: "We see things here that we could never describe, and you would never believe them if we did. I would not go back to Sweden if the whole country were presented to me."[19]

It is obvious that statements like these were topics of lively discussion in the cottages of Sweden. The astonished people naturally hungered for more information and some of them inquired of their "American" friends how the morals of this marvelous country compared with those of their own communities. Where everything was so great and rich and free, and the population was recruited from all parts of the world, how could the Americans be so honest, sympathetic, and kind as the letters pictured them? A correspondent in 1852 gave his explanation of the miracle. The country was large, he said, and the rascals were not concentrated in any one place; and if such persons did come to a community, they found no evil companions to add fuel to their baser instincts. Moreover, if they did not mend their ways, a volunteer committee of citizens would wait upon them and serve notice that they had the choice of leaving the community or submitting to arrest. The Americans would not brook violations of law, and therefore drunkenness, profanity, theft, begging, and dissension were so rare as to be almost entirely absent. This letter of recommendation did not stop here. It praised the observance of the Sabbath and asserted that the young people did not dance, drink, or play cards, as was the case in Sweden.[20]

Unlike the earlier travelers in America, who usually belonged to the upper classes in Europe, the emigrants found the moral standards on a much higher plane than in Sweden. During a residence of nine months in the new Utopia one emigrant had not heard of a single illegitimate child — yes, one case had actually come to his knowledge, and then a Swede was the offender. He found whisky-drinking very unusual and the advancement of temperance almost unbelievable. In a midwestern town of about two thousand inhabitants (the seat of a college with seven professors and 339 students) one had to be well acquainted in order to purchase whisky or strong wine. "From this incident you may judge of the state of temperance in American cities," he confided. After a residence of four years in southeastern Iowa, Peter Cassel testified that he had "dined in hundreds of homes," and had "yet to see a whiskey bottle on the table. This country suits me as a friend of temperance, but it is not suitable for the whiskey drinker."[21]

It is hardly conceivable that the Swedish immigrants were unanimously enthusiastic about temperance, whether voluntary or imposed by law, and the student of American social history would dot the map of mid-nineteenth-century America with thousands of oases; but it is nevertheless a fact that the Middle West, to which most of the immigrants gravitated, was in striking contrast to Sweden, where every landowning farmer operated a still and where the fiery *brännvin* at that time was as much a household necessity as coffee is today. Men, women, and children partook of its supposed health-giving properties in quantities appropriate to the occasion. To many immigrants who had heard the speeches or had read the tracts of the great apostles of temperance in Sweden, George Scott and Peter Wieselgren, and had patterned their lives after their precepts, the rural communities of Iowa, Illinois, Wisconsin, and Minnesota must have approached their ideal.

We must not be deluded into thinking that all the earlier Swedish immigrants were saints or models of virtue, but many of their letters bear testimony to the fact that there was profound dissatisfaction with the state of religion in Sweden. The writers had listened attentively to pietistic pastors and Baptist and lay preachers with sufficient courage to violate the conventicle act or to incur the displeasure of the church authorities, many of whom made merry over the flowing bowl and served Mammon rather than God. One cannot escape the conclusion that religion played a greater role in stimulating the desire to emigrate than writers have hitherto suspected; and if the student of immigration wishes to understand why the Swedes in America have turned away in such numbers from the church of their fathers in favor of other denominations or have held aloof from all church connections, he will find a study of religious conditions in the homeland a profitable one. It is by no means purely accidental that the beginnings of emigration coincide with the confluence of various forms of dissatisfaction with the state church.

The immigrants quickly sensed the difference between the pastors in America and Sweden. In 1849 a writer put it thus: "There are also Swedish preachers here who are so well versed in the Bible and in the correct interpretation that they seek the lost sheep and receive them again into their embrace and do not conduct themselves after the manner of Sweden, where the sheep must seek the shepherd and address him with high-sounding titles." Another requested his brother to send hymnbooks and catechisms, because the old copies were almost worn out with use. "We have a Swedish pastor. He . . . is a disciple of the esteemed Pastor Sellergren *[Peter Lorenz Sellergren, a prominent evan-*

gelistic pastor in Sweden]. . . . During the past eleven months he has preached every Sunday and holiday; on week days he works the same as the rest of us, because his remarkable preaching ability makes it unnecessary for him to write his sermons. One Sunday I heard him preach for over two hours, and he was as fluent the second hour as the first."[22]

A faithful disciple of the prophet Eric Janson drew an even sharper contrast between the two countries: "I take pen in hand, moved by the Holy Ghost, to bear witness to the things I have seen, heard, and experienced. We had a pleasant voyage . . . and I was not affected in the least with seasickness. . . . My words are inadequate to describe with what joy we are permitted daily to draw water from the well of life and how we have come to the land of Canaan, flowing with milk and honey, . . . which the Scriptures tell us the Lord has prepared for his people. He has brought us out of the devilish bondage of the ecclesiastical authorities, which still holds you in captivity. . . . Here we are relieved of hearing and seeing Sweden's satellites of the devil, whose tongues are inspired by the minions of hell and who murdered the prophets and Jesus himself and snatched the Bible from Eric Janson's hands and came against us with staves, guns, and torches, together with ropes and chains, to take away the freedom we have in Christ. But praised be God through all eternity that we are freed from them and are now God's peculiar people. . . . This is the land of liberty, where everybody can worship God in his own way and can choose pastors who are full of the Spirit, light, and perfection. . . . Therefore, make ready and let nothing hinder you . . . and depart from Babel, that is, Sweden, fettered body and soul by the law."[23]

The legal prohibition of conventicles and its consequences were fresh not only in the memory of fanatical Eric Jansonists but also in the mind of a former master shoemaker from Stockholm, who wrote: "The

American does not bother about the religious beliefs of his fellow men. It is the individual's own affair to worship God according to the dictates of his conscience, without interference from prelates clothed with power to prescribe what one must believe in order to obtain salvation. Here it is only a question of being a respectable and useful member of society."[24]

Another letter describes the situation in America as follows: "It is not unusual for men of meager education to witness for the truth with much greater blessing than the most learned preacher who has no religious experience. There are no statutes contrary to the plain teaching of the Word of God which prohibit believing souls from meeting for edification in the sacred truth of our Lord Jesus Christ."[25]

The sum and substance of the religious situation in America and Sweden is graphically stated in the words of an emigrant: "America is a great light in Christendom; there is a ceaseless striving to spread the healing salvation of the Gospel. The pastors are not lords in their profession, neither are they rich in the goods of this world. They strive to walk in the way God has commanded. They minister unceasingly to the spiritual and material welfare of men. There is as great difference between the pastors here and in Sweden as there is between night and day."[26]

One of the highly prized advantages America offered to the immigrant was the opportunity to rise from the lowest to the highest stratum of society. He found a land where the man whose hands were calloused by toil was looked upon as just as useful to society as the man in the white collar. The man who chafed under the cramped social conventions of Europe could not conceal his joy at finding a country where custom and tradition counted for little and where manual labor did not carry with it a social stigma. He had probably heard that the American people had elevated to the highest position of honor and trust such men of the people as Andrew Jackson and William Henry Harrison, but the actuality of the democracy in the "saga land" proved to be greater than the rumors that had kindled his imagination back home. And so he sat down to write about it to his countrymen, who read with astonishment that knew no bounds such statements as the following:

"The hired man, maid, and governess eat at the husbandman's table. Yes, sir,' says the master to the hand; 'yes, sir,' says the hand to the master. 'If you please, mam,' says the lady of the house to the maid; yes, madam,' replies the maid. On the street the maid is dressed exactly as the housewife. Today is Sunday, and at this very moment what do I see but a housemaid dressed in a black silk hat, green veil, green coat, and black dress, carrying a bucket of coal! This is not an unusual sight — and it is as it should be. All porters and coachmen are dressed like gentlemen. Pastor, judge, and banker carry market baskets."[27]

And read what a boon it was to live in a land where there were no laws minutely regulating trades and occupations and binding workers to terms of service: "This is a free country and nobody has a great deal of authority over another. There is no pride, and nobody needs to hold his hat in his hand for any one else. Servants are not bound for a fixed time. This is not Sweden, where the higher classes and employers have the law on their side so that they can treat their subordinates as though they were not human beings."[28]

The writer of this letter had probably felt the hard fist of his employer, because at that time physical chastisement was by no means unusual. If it was a great surprise to learn that a fine pedigree was not a requirement for admission to respectable society and to all classes of employment, no less sensational was the fact that the inhabitant of the western Canaan was not required to appear before an officer of the state to apply for a permit to visit another parish or to change his place of residence. In Sweden, of course, this official red tape was taken for granted, or its absence in America would not have called forth the following comment: "I am glad that I migrated to this land of liberty, in order to spare my children the slavish drudgery that was my lot; in this country if a laborer cannot get along with his employer, he can leave his job at any time, and the latter is obliged to pay him for the time he has put in at the same wage that was agreed upon for the month or year. We are free to move at any time and to any place without a certificate from the employer or from the pastor, because neither passports nor certificates are in use here."[29]

This newly won freedom was, in some cases, too rich for Swedish blood. One of the first pastors among the immigrants was rather disturbed about the conduct of some of his countrymen: "This political, religious, and economic freedom is novel and astonishing to the immigrant, who sees the spectacle of twenty-two millions of people ruling themselves in all orderliness. As a rule, the Swedes make use of this liberty in moderation, but a number act like calves that have been turned out to pasture. In most cases their cavorting is harmless, but sometimes they run amuck. They seem to think that a 'free country' gives them license to indulge in those things that are not in harmony with respect, uprightness, reliability, and veneration for the Word of God. . . . A rather characteristic incident illustrates this. A small boy, upon being reproved by his mother for appropriating a piece of cake, replied: 'Why, mother, aren't we in a free country now?'"[30] Making due allowance for the orthodox pessimism of a minister of the Gospel in every generation, historical research applied to certain Swedish settlements confirms the observations of this shepherd.

To a Swede, whose tongue was trained to flavor with cumbersome titles every sentence addressed to superiors and carefully to avoid any personal pronoun, the temptation to overwork the second person singular pronoun in

America was irresistible. The Swedish passion for high-sounding names and titles gave to the humbler members of society designations that magnified by contrast the grandeur of those applied to the elect. In his own country the Swede was shaved by Barber Johansson, was driven to his office by Coachman Petersson, conversed with Building Contractor Lundström, ordered Jeweler Andersson to make a selection of rings for his wife, and *skåled* with Herr First Lieutenant Silfversparre. There were even fine gradations of "titles" for the members of the rural population. Every door to the use of *du* was closed except in the most familiar conversation. The youngest member of the so-called better classes, however, might *dua* the man of toil, upon whose head rested the snows of many long Swedish winters. Can the sons of those humble folk in America be blamed for abusing the American privilege of using *du?* What a privilege to go into a store, the owner of which might be a millionaire, and allow one's hat to rest undisturbed! How much easier it was to greet the village banker with the salutation "Hello, Pete!" than to say "Good morning, Mr. Banker Gyllensvans!" "When I meet any one on the street, be he rich or poor, pastor or official, I never tip my hat when I speak," wrote an emigrant from Skåne in 1854. "I merely say 'Good day, sir, how are you?'"[31] On the other hand, what a thrill it was for the immigrant to be addressed as "mister" — the same title that adorned the American banker and lawyer and the first title he had ever had! "Mister" was much more dignified than "Jöns," "Lars," or "Per."

The equality that the law gives is not the equality of custom. The lack of political rights is comparatively easy to remedy, but social customs are harder to deal with because they are not grounded in law. From his birth the Swede was hampered by restrictive conventions which, though not always seen by the eye, were always felt by the emotions. The walls between the classes of society and various occupations were practically insurmountable. A person could not pass from a higher social class to an inferior one, even though the latter better became his nature or economic status, because that would be an everlasting disgrace. If a *bonde* had come into financial straits, the step down to the condition of a *torpare*[32] would have wrecked his spirit.

Class distinctions in America did not assert themselves in the same way; very often the foreman and laborer were neighbors, sat in the same pew, and belonged to the same lodge. One immigrant wrote of this in 1854 as follows: "Titles and decorations are not valued and esteemed here. On the other hand, efficiency and industry are, and the American sets a higher value on an intelligent workingman than on all the titles, bands, and stars that fall from Stockholm during an entire year. It will not do to be haughty and idle, *for that is not the fashion in this country, for it is to use the axe, the spade, and the saw and some other things to get money and not to be a lazy body.*"[33]

If the men appreciated the equality in dress and speech, the women were even more enthusiastic. In the old country married as well as unmarried women were labeled with titles of varying quality and their work was more masculine, judged by the American standard. In the "promised land" they were all classified simply as "Mrs." or "Miss," and the heavy, clumsy shoes and coarse clothing gave way to an attire more in keeping with the tastes and occupations of the "weaker sex." In Sweden the maid slept in the kitchen, shined shoes, and worked long hours; in America she had her own room, limited working hours, regular times for meals, and time to take a buggy ride with Ole Olson, who hailed from the same parish. If she had learned to speak English, she might even have a ride by the side of John Smith — and that was the height of ambition! And for all this she was paid five or six times as much as she had earned in Sweden. In letter after letter one finds expressions of astonishment and enthusiasm over this equality in conversation and dress. One writer relates that the similarity in dress between matron and maid was such that he could not distinguish between them until the latter's peasant speech betrayed her. It is easy to imagine the thorn of envy in the hearts of the women in Sweden when they learned how fortunate their American sisters were. Another letter contains the information that the duties of the maid were confined to indoor work in the country as well as in the city and that even milking was done by the men, an amusing sight to a Swede.

It is rather strange that there was not more serious complaint about the hard work that fell to the lot of the immigrants. It is true that more than one confessed that they did not know what hard work was until they came to America, but there was a certain pride in the admission. It was probably the American optimism that sustained their spirits. They saw everything in the light of a future, where the "own farm" plus a bank account was the ultimate goal. This feeling of independence and self-confidence was also heightened by the vast distances of the Middle West, its large farms, billowing prairies, and cities springing up like magic.[34] In contrast with the small-scale agriculture and the tiny hamlets of his native parish, the immigrant felt that he was a part of something great, rich, and mighty, the possibilities of which were just beginning to be exploited. Said a Swedish farmer in 1849: "Here in Illinois is room for the entire population of Sweden. During the present winter I am certain that more grass has been burned than there is hay in the entire kingdom of Sweden... The grass now is just half grown, and the fields give the appearance of an ocean, with a house here and there, separated by great distance."[35]

The Swede who came to the Mississippi Valley found a frontier society, with many institutions in advance of those of an older society and without the multitude of officials that strutted and blustered in Sweden. In fact, as one immigrant wrote, he was hardly conscious of living under a government, and the system of taxation fooled him into thinking that there were no taxes at all. The salary of the president of the United States was a mere pittance compared with the income of the royal family — a fact not omitted in the letters.[36]

Not a few of the "America letters" go to extremes in setting forth contrasts between "poverty-ridden Sweden" and the rich and mighty republic. Here is an example: "We hope and pray that the Lord may open the eyes of Svea's people that they might see their misery: how the poor workingman is despised and compelled to slave, while the so-called better classes fritter away their time and live in luxury, all of which comes out of the pockets of the miserable workingmen. . . .We believe that all the workers had better depart and leave the lords and parasites to their fate. There is room here for all of Svea's inhabitants."[37]

Quotations from the "America letters" could be multiplied to show the reaction of the Swedish immigrants to the American environment, but a sufficient number have been presented to demonstrate that they were unusually responsive to the impressions that rushed upon them soon after they had cast their lot with their brothers and sisters from Great Britain, Ireland, Germany, Norway, and Holland. And not only that, but their letters remain to record the fact that in America they found a society that nearly approached their conception of an ideal state. This explains why students of immigration agree almost unanimously that the Swedes assimilated more rapidly and thoroughly than any other immigrant stock. After all, why should anyone be hesitant about taking out naturalization papers in the land of Canaan? Some letters written by men who had scarcely time enough to unpack their trunks read like Fourth of July orations: "As a son of the great republic which extends from ocean to ocean, I will strive to honor my new fatherland. A limitless field is opened for the development of Swedish culture and activity. Destiny seems to have showered its blessings on the people of the United States beyond those of any other nation in the world."[38]

The Sweden of 1840—60 is no more and the America of Abraham Lincoln belongs to the ages; but for hundreds of thousands of people in the land of the midnight sun America, in spite of the geographical distance, lies closer to them than the neighboring province. In some parts of Sweden the "America letters" from near relatives brought Chicago closer to them than Stockholm. They knew more about the doings of their relatives in Center City, Minnesota, than about Uncle John in Jönkoping.

In deciphering an "America letter" the historian is prone to forget the anxious mother who for months — perhaps years — had longed for it, and the letter that never came is entirely missing from the archives and newspaper columns. But if he turns the musty pages of the Swedish-American newspapers, his eyes will fall on many advertisements similar to the following: "Our dear son Johan Anton Petersson went to America last spring. We have not heard a line from him. If he sees this advertisement, will he please write to his people in Sweden? We implore him not to forget his aged parents and, above all, not to forget the Lord."[39]

If many letters were stained with tears in the little red cottages in Sweden, there were not a few written by trembling hands in the log cabins of Minnesota and later in the sod houses of Nebraska. And sometimes the heart was too full to allow the unsteady hand to be the only evidence of longing for parents and brothers and sisters, as the following quotation reveals: "I will not write at length this time. Nothing of importance has happened, and if you come, we can converse.

God alone knows whether that day will ever dawn — my eyes are dimmed with tears as I write about it. What a happy day it would be if, contrary to all expectations, we children could see our parents."[40] Miraculous things happened in the land of Canaan; it could transform a conservative Swedish *bonde* into a "hundred per cent American" in spirit, but it could not so easily sever the ties of blood. Neither could the storm-tossed Atlantic prevent sisters, cousins, uncles, and aunts from accepting invitations embalmed in "America letters" to attend family reunions in the land of Canaan.

FOOTNOTES

[1] This paper, read on June 14, 1929, at the Hutchinson session of the eighth state historical convention, is based mainly upon documentary materials discovered in Sweden by the author.

[2] *Nya Wexjö-Bladet* (Vaxjo), May 22, 1869.

[3] Papers like *Aftonbladet* (Stockholm), *Östgötha Correspondenten* (Linköping, *Norrlands-Posten* (Gävle), and *Jönköpings-Bladet* and writers like Karl J. L. Almqvist and Pehr Thomasson foreshadowed a new day in religion, politics, society, and economics.

[4] *Jönköpings-Bladet,* May 26, 1846.

[5] For *a* sketch of Cassel and a reprint of his letters, see George M. Stephenson, "Documents Relating to Peter Cassel and the Settlement at New Sweden, Iowa," in the *Swedish-American Historical Bulletin,* 2:1—82 (February, 1929).

[6] "There is peace and prosperity here. I have come in contact with millions of people of all sorts and conditions, but I have never heard of dissension, and we have never been snubbed. There are black and brown people, but all are friendly and agreeable." Letter from Samuel Jönsson, Buffalo, New York, November 22, 1846, in *Östgötha Correspondenten,* May 26, 1847.

[7] This letter, dated February 9, 1846, was published in *Östgötha Correspondenten* on May 16, 1846. It is reprinted, with English translation, in the *Swedish-American Historical Bulletin, 2:22—28, 55—62* (February, 1929). The abundance of fish and game was mentioned frequently in letters to the old country. See, for example, a letter from A. M. D--m, Taylors Falls, Minnesota, in *Östgötha Correspondenten,* July 27, 30, 1853.

[8] Correspondence from Döderhultsvik to *Kalmar-Posten,* April 23, 1852; *Landskroa Nya Tidning,* cited in *Barås Tidning,* June 13, *1854; Hwad Nytt?* (Eksjö), February 18, 1869; *Wäktaren,* cited in *Dalpilen* (Falun), July 17, 1869;Aron Edström, "Blad ur svensk-amerikanska

banbrytarelifvets historia," in *Svensk-amerikanska kalendern,* 61—64 (Worcester, Massachusetts, 1882).

[9] "His first letter was dated at Milwaukee, Wisconsin Territory, October 15, 1841, and published in *Aftonbladet,* January 4, 5, 1842; his second letter was dated at New Upsala, Wisconsin, January 23, 1842, and published in *Aftonbladet,* May 28, 30, 31, June 3, 7, 9, 1842.

[10] "Letters dated January 18, 1841, and July 4, 1842, in *Aftonbladet,* April 6, October 6, 13, 1842.

[11] "Letter dated February 10, 1843, in *Skara Tidning,* May 18, 1843. Unonius mentions the meeting with Friman in his *Minnen från en sjuttonårig vistelse i nordvestra Amerika,* 1:182 (Upsala, 1861).

[12] "Letter dated February 10, 1843, in *Skara Tidning,* May 18, 1843.

[13] "Letter from J. C. Melander, Eksjö, June 27, 1843, in *Skara Tidning,* July 13, 1843.

[14] "Extracts from several letters in *Skara Tidning,* November 2, 1843.

[15] "*Emigrationsutredningen,* 7:131—263 (Stockholm, 1908).

[16] Peter Cassel to relatives and friends, December 13, 1848, in the *Swedish American Historical Bulletin,* 2:78 (February, 1929).

[17] Letter from Johan Johansson, Burlington, Iowa, November 12, 1849, in *Östgötha Correspondenten,* April 5, 1850. Compare the following statement in a letter from Stephan Stephanson, May 17, 1854: "There is no class distinction here, but all are equals, and not as in Sweden, where the working people are looked down upon and are called 'the rabble,' whereas the lazy gentlemen are called 'better folk.'" This manuscript is in the author's possession.

[18] "Steffan Steffanson to relatives and friends, October 9, 1849, in Swedish Historical Society of America, *Yearbooks,* 11:86—100 (St. Paul, 1926).

[19] Unsigned letters from New York in *Norrlands-Posten,* December 29, 1856; and from Chicago, September 9, 1853, in *Nya Wexjö-Bladet,* October 7, 1853.

[20] Unsigned letter, dated January 23, 1852, in *Bibel-Wännen* (Lund), September, 1852.

[21] L. P. Esbjörn to Peter Wieselgren, Andover, Illinois, May 23, 1850, a manuscript in the *Stadsbibliotek* of Gothenburg; Cassel to relatives and friends, December 13, 1848, in the *Swedish-American Historical Bulletin,* 2:81 (February, 1929).

[22] Steffan Steffanson to relatives and friends, October 9, 1849, in Swedish Historical Society of America, *Yearbooks,* 11:97; Peter Cassel to relatives and friends, December 13, 1848, in the *Swedish-American Historical Bulletin,* 2:75.

[23] Letter from Anders Jonsson, Bishop Hill, Illinois, February 9, 1847, in *Hudikswalls-Weckoblad,* July 17, 1847.

[24] Letter from Erik Hedström, Southport, Wisconsin, in *Aftonbladet,* September 20, 1843.

[25] Letter from Jon Andersson in *Norrlands-Posten,* January 12, 1852.

[26] Letter from Åke Olsson, Andover, Illinois, February 20, 1850, in *Norrlands-Posten,* June 3, 1850.

[27] Letter from New York in *Aftonbladet,* reprinted in *Barometern* (Kalmar), June 5, 1852.

[28] Letter from Åke Olsson, Andover, Illinois, February 20, *1850, in Norrlands-Posten,* June 3, 1850.

[29] Letter from Stephan Stephanson, May 17, 1854.

[30] Letter from L. P. Esbjörn, Andover, Illinois, May 6, 1850, in *Norrlands-Posten,* June 20, 1850.

[31] *Carlshamns Allehanda,* August 3, 1854. Anders Andersson, who for some time after his emigration corresponded with a crown official in Norrland, soon changed his style of address from *ni* to *du.* See his letters edited by Anna Söderblom, "Läsare och Amerikafarare på 1840-talet," in *Julhelg,* 80—93 (Stockholm, 1925).

[32] "Renter" suggests the meaning.

[33] Unsigned letter from Chicago, August 3, 1854, in *Skånska Posten,* reprinted in *Carlshamns Allehanda,* October 4, 1854.

[34] Letter to *Götheborgs Handels- och Sjöfarts-Tidning,* April 22, 23, 1852.

[35] "Letter of O. Bäck, Victoria, Illinois, in *Norrlands-Posten,* April 3, 1849.

[36] *Götheborgs Handels- och Sjöfarts-Tidning,* April 22, 23, 1852.

[37] "letter from Åke Olsson, Andover, Illinois, February 20, 1850, in *Norrlands-Posten,* June 3, 1850.

[38] letter from C. P. Agrelius, New York, April 14, 1849, in *Östgötha Correspondenten,* July 4, 1849.

[39] *Chicago-Bladet,* January 13, 1885.

[40] Mary H. Stephenson to her relatives, November 3, 1867, in Swedish Historical Society of America, *Yearbooks,* 7:90 (St. Paul, 1922).

This article originally appeared in *The Swedish Historical Society of America Yearbook, VII* (1922) 33-52. Reprinted by Permission.

SOME FOOTNOTES TO THE HISTORY OF SWEDISH IMMIGRATION FROM ABOUT 1855 TO ABOUT 1865

By GEORGE M. STEPHENSON

(Assistant Professor of History in the University of Minnesota)

Emigration from Sweden to America began in earnest in the decade of the fifties, although it was not until after the close of the Civil war that Swedish-America received its greatest additions. Prior to 1850 little was known about Sweden and its inhabitants in the United States. Gustaf Unonius, who led the vanguard of Swedish immigrants, states that all Europeans who spoke neither English, French nor Dutch were Germans in the eyes of Americans.[1] It must have hurt the pride of the Swedes who enlisted in the federal army to hear themselves referred to as "Dutch" by American comrades associated with them in the war to Preserve the union.[2] A Swedish Lutheran clergyman, journeying up the Mississippi river to Minnesota in 1855, was surprised to find himself labeled a Swedenborgian by a fellow traveler who had been informed that he was a Swedish minister.[3]

1) Gustaf Unonius, *Minnen fran en sjuttonårig vistelse i Nordrestra Amerika* (2 vols., Upsala, 1861, 1862), 1: 31.
2) Letter of Captain Arosenius from Little Rock, Arkansas, November 9, 1864, in *Hemlandet* (Chicago, Ill.), November 23, 1864.
3) *Hemlandet* (Galesburg Ill.), March 31, 1855.

After 1850 the columns of the newspapers in Sweden and the relatively few Swedish language papers in America contain abundant evidence that the forces which had initiated and accelerated the movement of population from England, Ireland, Germany, and the Netherlands were developing similar results in Scandinavia.[4] Hard times, crop failures, difficulty of securing loans, money stringency, low wages, men out of work, the demand for laborers and housemaids due to the American civil war, the federal immigration law of 1864, a certain dissatisfaction with church and state, the propaganda of states and emigration agencies, letters from enthusiastic immigrants,

---

4) *Hemlandet,* the first Swedish newspaper in the United States, was established at Galesburg, Illinois, January 3, 1855, by the able and energetic Rev. T. N. Hasselquist, perhaps the most influential and best beloved man among Swedish-Americans. In 1858 the publication office was removed to Chicago, when Mr. Hasselquist relinquished the editorship. May 4, 1855, the editor announced that the subscribers totaled some 600, adding that he saw no reason why the Swedes could not have as good a paper with as large a circulation as the Norwegians. He estimated the number of Swedes in the United States between 60,000 and 80,000. On March 1, 1856, the circulation had almost reached 1,000. The value of this paper as a source for the history of Swedish immigration during the years under review can hardly be overemphasized. Almost every issue contains extracts from papers published in Sweden, letters from immigrants in widely scattered communities, information about Swedish settlements, prices of land, Increase of population, fertility of soil, departure of immigrant parties from Sweden, and arrival of groups of immigrants in America. The editorial announcement in English (March 12, 1855) reads as follows: "We take the liberty to send this Swedish paper to the editors of several English and German papers, in hopes that they will have the goodness to exchange with us. They will in most cases find persons that are able to read our paper, and to inform them what sort of sentiments we advocate and spread among the foreign population of this country. Our present terms are $1 a year, and we are willing to pay the difference In price to those exchanges who desire us to do so."

all stirred the blood of the adventurous, ambitious, and liberty-loving sons of "gamla Svea" until the "America fever" ravaged parish after parish.

In Sweden, as in many other countries of Europe, the Increasing numbers of those who were eager to surrender their birthright in favor of citizenship in the great republic across the Atlantic awakened alarm in certain quarters, and the utmost efforts were employed to stem the tide of emigration. Almost without exception the newspapers of Sweden painted America in the blackest colors.[5] Every obstacle and every disappointment in America that could be culled from letters were compiled and published. *Nya Wexjö-Bladet* said that if the public knew how many emigrants were unfortunate, America would not be thought of as the promised land.[6] *Nerikes Allehanda* prints a letter from "one of the workmen fooled to go to America," who charges that the literature circulated in Sweden about America is full of lies. He complains of the hot weather, hard work, expensive clothes, high railroad fares, and the way Americans exploit the Swedes. He found no rich prairies—only hills and valleys. He threatens an emigration

---

5) *Hemlandet,* January 28 and August 12, 1857; February 8 and December 20, 1865. The editor of *Hemlandet* doubted that these exaggerations served their purpose. He wrote that he had lived among the immigrants over four years. had traveled quite extensively, and deemed himself familiar with conditions. Swedes have greater opportunities in America, and this is more true of the west than of the east. People in Sweden would be astonished at some of the homes of immigrants. A neatly made bed, with snow white linen and pretty quilt, a table and rocking chair, well carpeted floors, and wives dressed as ladies immediately meet the eye.

6) *Hemlandet,* August 12, 1857.

agent with "en påhälsning" if he remains in Sweden.[7] The argument was set forth that if the Swedes worked as hard in the old country as in the new, their circumstances would he as good. Gustaf Unonius, who had spent seventeen years in America before returning to his native land, enlisted in the ranks of the anti-American propagandists. In a letter printed in a Stockholm paper, while denying hostility to America, he seeks to dissuade prospective emigrants—they ought to wait at least a year. He cites the civil war, copperhead troubles, and Indian uprisings.[8] The outbreak of the civil war was a welcome opportunity for the enemies of America. The advertisements and literature of emigration agents were denounced as tricks to secure recruits for the federal army.[9] Reports were circulated that accurate information about the progress of the war for the preservation of the union were not forthcoming because of the censorship of the American press;[10] and when the news of the

---

[7] *Hemlandet,* December 20, 1865. Commenting on this letter, *Hemlandet* says that emigrants are easily fooled, because they have heard so much about high wages and believe anything they are told. They ought to understand that they cannot command the highest wages until they have resided here for a time.

[8] Letter to *Nya Dagliga Allehanda,* printed in *Hemlandet* April 15, 1863. The editor of *Hemlandet* doubts the writer's good faith and says he is misinformed. Where does he get his information? he asks. Out of the air, or from copperheads?

[9] *Hemlandet,* May 4, 1864. The editor denied that such methods were employed by the American government. He was inclined to attribute the source of the alleged information to such enemies of the government as the *Scandinavisk Post* of New York.

[10] *Hemlandet,* March 1, 1865. To disprove this charge *Hemlandet* advises the Swedish editors to read certain American papers. If America were Europe, he writes, the press would be censored.

assassination of Abraham Lincoln came, it was accepted as a harbinger of further disorder: that the incompetency of Andrew Johnson would necessitate the appointment of a military dictator.[11]

Perhaps the most effective ally of the press in the work of discrediting America was the pulpit.[12] If the statements of immigrants may be credited, the spectacle of ministers in the pulpit referring to immigrants as "unfaithful Sons" and "traitors was by no means unusual. Frequently when emigrants applied for letters of dismission pastors seized the opportunity of reading a lecture on the error of their way Kyrkowännen reports the substance of the proceedings of a meeting attended by nine ministers and five laymen at which the question of sending pastors to America was discussed.[13] The sentiment was unanimous that the need of pastors to minister to the spiritual wants of their erring countrymen was great; but five ministers insisted that the need in Sweden was fully as urgent, that the immigrants have their Bibles, and that, having departed voluntarily and for the sake of money, they were entitled to no sympathy. The editor of Kyrkowännen adds that it would he impossible for Swedish ministers to establish an episcopate, because the president of the United States is the head of neither the Lutheran nor any other church. In 1858 the editor of Hemlandet was sorry to inform his readers that there was little or no hope of securing ministers from Sweden. The only solution of the problem was the establishment of educational institutions to train pastors in the land of adoption. Even in this undertaking no assistance was immediately forthcoming from abroad.

---

11) *Hemlandet,* June 7, 1865.
12) *Hemlandet,* February 8, 1865.
13) *Hemlandet,* November 21, 1856.

A petition from the Evangelical Lutheran Synod of Northern Illinois to the king of Sweden for a collection in the churches in his kingdom in behalf of an endowment fund for the Scandinavian professorship at Illinois State University was denied.[14]

The Swedish government and the officials of the government quite naturally discouraged a movement which sapped the vitality of the nation by taking away the flower of its peasant population. About 1840 the laws regulating emigration were made somewhat more liberal,[15] but on January 1, 1865, a more stringent policy went into effect.[16] Immigrants who upon their arrival in America found themselves in unfortunate circumstances received little sympathy from the Swedish consuls who felt themselves under no obligation to assist people who of their own accord abandoned a country where conditions were more favorable.[17]

Unfortunately there was an element of truth in the charges of the press, clergy, and government officials. All too frequently emigration agents stopped short of nothing to produce results. Their advertisements painted America

---

14) *Hemlandet,* May 11, 1859. The editor (May 18, 1859) deplored the action of the king. He wrote that the Swedes in the United States are no longer Swedish subjects, but are nevertheless children of the Lutheran church and cherish a warm feeling for Sweden and the king.

15) George T. Flom, "The Early Swedish Immigration to Iowa," in *Iowa Journal of History and Politics,* (October,1905), 3: 593,94.

16) Letter from Rev. L. P. Esbjörn, dated June 21, 1865, In *Hemlandet,* July 26, 1865. *Hemlandet* says that the purpose of the regulations is to discourage emigration, but that the result will he that emigrants for the most part will depart from England and Germany. Norway is wiser: It does not like emigration, but wants to carry the emigrants In its own ships.

17) *Hemlandet,* August 27, 1857, and August 16, 1865.

in the brightest colors without a single shadow. Few if any immigrants could command the wages promised until they had become familiar with the language and customs of the land. The wages quoted were often reckoned in depreciated currency,—a most serious misrepresentation. Prospective emigrants were incapable of taking in the vast distances of the American continent, for the agents told them nothing about the cost of arriving at their destinations. Apparently many immigrants expected to step into smiling wheat fields a stone's throw from Castle Garden. For these reasons more than one immigrant family upon landing was penniless, without shelter and friendly advice and assistance. The lands advertised were often poor and inaccessible, far removed from other settlements, augmenting the trials and discouragements which usually accompanied the immigrants' first years in America. There was considerable complaint in Sweden about the activity of Mormon missionaries, and more than one Swede came to America a convert to Mormonism with little or no real conception of the true nature of that religion and of the conditions in their western colony.[18]

Castle Garden, the Ellis Island of that day, swarmed with sharks and runners who preyed upon the credulity of

---

[18] The sources for this paragraph are as follows: *Hemlandet*, January 3 and July 28, 1855; October 12, 1859; June 10, 1863; letter of Anders Ståhl, Carver, Minnesota, "Till Landsmän i Swerige om deras utflyttning," in *Ibid.*, June 21, 1865; *Ibid.*, July 5 and 25, 1865; *Göteborgs Handelstidning,* and *Göteborgs Posten,* In *Ibid.*, May 15 and 29, 1866; *ibid.,* July 3 and 17 and Septemter 18, 1866; *Emigranten* (Norwegian, Madison, Wisconsin), October 17, 1864, and May 2, 1859. Rev. L. P. Esbjörn wrote from Sweden *(Hemlandet,* August 9, 1865) that at a "prestmöte" at Upsala he took the opportunity of sounding a warning against the agents who were attempting to stimulate emigration.

immigrants, insinuating themselves into their confidence, stealing from them, cheating them at exchange, and sending them to wrong destinations. A Swedish Lutheran missionary at New York, Rev. A. Andreen, wrote to *Hemlandet* in 1865 that there were between twenty and thirty Swedes at Castle Garden without a cent to take them farther, begging for bread and imploring him to write letters to their friends and relatives for money to save them from the poor house. He rendered assistance to a Swedish Finn family detained at Castle Garden for two weeks, whose trunk containing clothes, some silver, and fifty-five dollars had been stolen.[19]

A most tragic story can be pieced together from the columns of *Hemlandet* during the years 1865 and 1866. On the twenty-fourth of August, 1865, the Richmond, Virginia, correspondent of a Baltimore paper saw the unusual sight of about a hundred Swedes,—men, women, and children,—surrounded by gesticulating negroes, waiting for a boat to take them to Goochland county, Virginia.[20] The negroes, as ignorant of the immigrants' circumstances as the latter were of the English language, sought to dissuade them from coming south to fill the places formerly occupied by slaves. These Richmond Swedes had a variety of experiences, the details in some cases being related in a simple, graphic manner in a number of letters to *Hemlandet*.

It appears that a small party of Swedes were induced

---

[19] *Hemlandet,* September 20 and October 18, 1865.
[20] *Hemlandet* (September 13, 1865) clipped this account from *Sändebudet*. The editor of the latter paper wondered how the Swedes got down there.

to go to Richmond by a Swedish resident of that city, a certain Mr. Ericksson, who secured satisfactory employment for them with a Doctor Walker. Mr. Ericksson saw an opportunity to make money, so he organized a company, and, provided with alluring bait in the form of glowing letters signed by Swedes on the Walker place, set out for New York. The well dressed man readily gained recruits among his immigrant countrymen, some of whom were penniless and easily taken in.

Those whose destination was Minnesota, Iowa, or Chicago were told that, while he could not take them to the designated place, he could promise them excellent wages in communities close by,— perhaps a journey of two or three hours. Some signed year contracts by which the men were to receive $150 and board, the women $100, and children under fifteen who could do light work, food and clothing. Even more liberal inducements were offered when circumstances demanded.[21]

At Richmond one party while waiting for the canal boat

---

21) Letter from Olof Brink, Goochland county, to his cousin Olof at Swede Bend (now Madrid), Iowa, in *Hemlandet,* October 18, 1865; Carl Hammarström, Richmond, to Swenson, in *Ibid.,* November 1, 1865; *Ibid.,* November 8, 1865; editor's conversation with one of the Richmond Swedes at Chicago, in *Ibid.,* November 29, 1865; letter containing extracts from letters from two Richmond Swedes to writer at Marine Mills, Minnesota, in *Ibid.,* January 2, 1866; letter from man who acted as interpreter for returned Richmond family, in *Ibid.,* January 23, 1866; three column letter from Jamestown, New York, by G. Kyllander, one of the Richmond party, in *Ibid.,* March 13, 1866. About the middle of August, 1865, in a conversation with the editor of *Hemlandet* (August 16, 1865), C. J. Halléen of Chicago told about an agent for a colonization company in Virginia trying to lure Immigrants to that state. He said they were promised work for a year, with three days labor per week, five acres of land, a horse and a cow, plus $100. Halléen did not know whether any Swedes went.

slept out of doors in a pouring rain. Tired and wet, they carried their trunks and luggage to the miserable boat and to the plantations. Their lodgings were filthy slave shanties. After toiling under the hot August sun from sunrise to sundown, their food consisted of pancakes and wormy pork, and the hard floor was their bed. After working eleven weeks a man and wife were paid in worthless Confederate money.

The unfortunate immigrants appealed through letters to friends and relatives for financial assistance to enable them to leave the south. These letters were given wide circulation through *Hemlandet.* Money was subscribed by individuals and congregations, but how many members of the colony were left stranded in the south does not appear from the record.

The Swedes who arrived in the decade of the fifties found the public mind agitated by two great issues: slavery and know-nothingism. Unonius was so impressed with the majesty of American citizenship that he refrained from active participation in politics.[22] He was severely critical of the Germans and Irish, who, he says, rushed into American affairs before they were familiar with conditions. Slavery and nativism, however, vitally affected the fortunes of the foreign-born, and almost immediately they were swept into the political whirl-pool.

One of the first issues of *Hemlandet* contained an editorial, on "Know Nothingismen."[23] The editor regarded the organization of the know-nothing party as an attempt on the part of southern politicians to split the political power

---

22) Unonius, *Minnen,* 1: 335.
23) *Hemlandet,* March 31, 1855.

the north. He admitted that the patience of native Americans had been sorely tried by the critical attitude toward American institutions and laws assumed by the German radicals and Catholics, but he could not sanction the methods of the know-nothings. Secret organizations are foreign to a republic, and their methods belong more to Russia than to a free people. He charged that the nativist papers tried to find all the faults of the immigrants and to deal with them as though they were thieves, drunkards, and rowdies. As for the Swedes, Norwegians, and Danes, continued the editorial, they were too few in number to have had much influence either for good or evil. Almost everywhere they were looked upon as industrious peoples.

The democratic and the newly organized republican party in their appeals for the votes of the Swedish naturalized citizens tried to pin the stigma of know-nothingism on one another. In editorials and letters to *!Hemlandet* it was admitted that in the past the democrats had favored foreigners, but in later years the democracy had degraded itself by affiliating with the slave power and those interests which had opposed the best interests of immigrants by defeating a liberal homestead bill and espousing measures designed to curtail the rights of naturalized citizens.[24]

---

[24] Editorial In *Hemlandet,* September 12, 1856; letter from Galesburg, Ill., *Ibid.,* September 8, 1855; letter from Westpoint, Indiana, *Ibid.,* August 29, 1856; letter from La fayette, Indiana, *Ibid.,* August 29, 1856. Referring editorially to democratic opposition to Representative Galusha Grow's amendment reserving the public lands for actual settlers for ten years after they were offered for sale, *Hemlandet* (February 1, 1859) asks: "Isn't this conclusive evidence that the south and the northern democrats always oppose every measure in the interest of the free white laborer? How beneficial

The Swedish immigrants could not reconcile the liberty-loving professions of the democratic administration and democratic papers with their sympathetic attitude towards Russia in the Crimean war.[25] Knowing Russia's encroachments on Sweden and the cruel persecution of Finland, the Swedes saw in the Crimean war a struggle between the righteousness of Great Britain and France and the despotism of Russia. *Hemlandet* attributed American sympathy for Russia to the old grudge against England, the Czar's hypocritical catering to certain influential Americans, and the natural leaning of the slave power in control of the Pierce administration toward despotism.

In the campaign of 1856 indications are that the Swedes generally supported Fremont, the republican candidate, as against Buchanan and Fillmore, the candidates of the

---

would not this measure be for our poor countrymen in Minnesota and other new states?" Reverend Andrew .Jackson wrote from Meeker county, Minnesota, *(Hemlandet,* October 12, *1859)* that the Swedish farmers in that vicinity were worried over the prospective public land sales, and that those who had cattle intended to sell their last cow to prevent their pre emption claims from being bought from under them. Those who had no land were not so worried, because they could go sixty or a hundred miles farther west, where there is plenty of unclaimed land. There they could await the incoming of a liberal administration which will assure the enactment of a law granting free lands to actual settlers. One settler suggested that the settlers should go *en masse* to the land office and with weapons in hand frighten any one who might bid on land. Another suggested that they go to the Big Woods to gather ginseng. A third had in mind to take his old oxen and hand-made wagon, fill It with blackbirds. and, clad in wooden shoes and deer skin cap, go to Washington to inform the old man In the White house that he was a farmer from Minnesota, who desired to sell *willebråd* in order to pay for his land.

25)*Hemlandet,* June 6, August 8, and September 8, 1855.

democratic and American party respectively. At a meeting of Scandinavians in Chicago resolutions were adopted condemning slavery, the Kansas policy of the administration, and the principles of the know-nothing party as unjust to foreigners and inciting hatred between natives and immigrants, and declaring in favor of free speech and press, the republican national platform and candidates, and the Illinois state republican ticket.[26]

The Swedes were so ardently opposed to the extension of slavery that only the most pronounced know-nothing planks in republican platforms could have kept them out of the party. The liberal republican platforms in the states harboring the bulk of Swedish immigrants refuted the democratic charges that the republicans were hostile to adopted citizens. In a letter addressed to the Swedes in Minnesota written by Reverend P. A. Cederstam, from Chisago Lake, printed in *Hemlandet,* September 19, 1857, he says that he was a member of the republican state constitutional convention. There were two rival conventions, says he, democratic and republican, which drew up separate constitutions. The republicans had a chance to show their supposed hostility to immigrants, but when the chairman appointed the committee to formulate the article on suffrage, he appointed three Europeans and two Americans, and made the writer, who had been in America only four years, chairman. Was this know-nothingism? asks Cedarstam. When the article in question was discussed in open convention, most of the Americans were in favor of making no distinction between natives and foreign-born.

In the election of 1860 the slavery issue was so clean-cut that the Swede who voted against Abraham Lincoln

---

26) *Hemlandet,* August 15 and 29, 1856.

was arare specimen.

Fortunately or unfortunately, the Swedes are as susceptible to environment as other peoples. Svante Palm, who was among the earliest Swedish immigrants and who settled near Austin, Texas, in 1855 wrote to the editor of *Hemlandet* that he could not indorse all the sentiments voiced in his editorials.[27] We agree on know-nothingism, wrote Palm, but on slavery we hold entirely different opinions. We live in a slave state and are in daily contact with masters and slaves. We find the slaves better treated than the working classes in Sweden. Some of us Swedes own slaves and all want to own them as soon as we can. Our countrymen in the northern states write that they are treated worse 'than slaves. The abolitionists in the north are fanatics. We citizens of a slave state are good, *renhåriga* democrats and believe in state rights.

Palm's letter aroused much criticism among Swedish-Americans. The editor of *Hemlandet* received many letters expressing surprise that a Swede would defend the institution of slavery.[28] A letter from Texas assured him that not all of Palm's countrymen shared his sympathy with slavery. He knew of not a single Swede around Austin who had purchased a slave, although many were able financially. He admitted that wages in Sweden were poor, but saw no comparison between the condition of the laboring classes in that country and the slaves in the south.

---

27) *Hemlandet,* August 28, 1855.
28) *Hemlandet,* October 20 and November 10, 1855. For interesting letters about Swedish settlers and settlements in Texas, see *Hemlandet,* August 27, 1857, and July 24, 1866.

Sad experiences were in store for Svante Palm with the outbreak of the civil war. At the close of the war a Swedish resident of Texas dropped into the *Hemlandet* office and informed the editor that his old friend and correspondent who had employed his talents to defend slavery had learned a lesson, had deserted the cause of slavery, and was a strong union man. The informant stated that many Swedes were drafted into the confederate army, but some of them took advantage of the first opportunity to desert to the union army.[29]

For the years of the civil war the files of *Hemlandet* are a source of no small importance. Almost every issue contains letters from Swedish soldiers at the front, giving accounts of battles, conditions in the south, the numbers of Swedes in certain companies, and exhortations to their countrymen to give loyal support to the government. *Hemlandet* gave warm support to the war and was an ardent admirer of President Lincoln. Frequent warnings were sounded against the propaganda of the copperheads and peace democrats, who held up the substitute clause of the conscription act before the Swedes as a classic example of the despotic nature of the republican administration. This feature of the law disturbed a number, but *Hemlandet* sought to dispel their fears by pointing to the fact that in the old country a substitute could be hired. The editor had no sympathy for the German immigrants who agitated against the law and made odious comparisons with the Prussian military system which their leaders sought to escape in 1848.[30]

---

29) *Hemlandet,* June 21, 1865.

30) *Hemlandet,* March 11 and 18 and April 1 and 8, 1868. In Chicago certain Swedes organized the "Philadelphia" society. the purpose of which was to establish a common treasury from which to pay substitutes for those in the society who might be drafted. Each

The Swedes in various parts of the country were anxious to advertise the loyalty of their countrymen. They wrote letters giving results of elections, in which the Swedish vote went overwhelmingly in favor of republican candidates and in support of a vigorous prosecution of the war.[31)]

The historian who aspires to write a comprehensive history of the Swedes in America will have to make a diligent study of the many letters to *!Hemlandet* from

---

member was required to pay $100 into the treasury. If no member were drafted, the sum would be returned, and any surplus remaining after the required substitutes were hired, would be divided among the members.—*Hemlandet,* September 7, 1864.

31) The following data (the present writer does not vouch for the accuracy) is taken from correspondence to *Hemlandet* for 1864. In Goodhue, Minnesota, Lincoln received 59 votes to 21 for "Gunboat" McClellan. The Irish and Germans voted for McClellan because they wanted the price of whiskey reduced (November 23). In Burlington, Iowa, every Swede with one exception voted for Lincoln (November 23). Knoxville, Illinois: Lincoln received 70 to 2 for McClellan. "How many Swedish communities can beat that?" (November 30). In Rockford, Illinois, McClellan received not a single Swedish vote (December 7). In Holden, Minnesota, populated entirely by Scandinavians, out of 141 votes only 1 was democratic. In town of Cannon Falls, Minnesota,—which the Americans used to call the "democratic town,"—the Swedish farmers carried the union ticket (December 7, 1864). In Jamestown, New York, every Swede voted the union ticket. In the town of Sugar Grove, Warren county, Pennsylvania, every Swede voted for Lincoln. "The Swedes are all right, say the 'yankee'" (January 1, 1865). It appears that in certain Swedish communities in Illinois a Mr. Lange, who called himself a Swede, exerted himself in behalf of the democratic cause in 1864. According to *Hemlandet,* some copperheads had assembled on the west side of Chicago to organize a Scandinavian democratic club. A doubting Thomas moved that the Scandinavians present should arise; and when only five arose, the meeting adjourned to a nearby wine cellar for a glass of beer or two (October 12, 1864).

Swedish settlements. The limits of this paper will not allow an extensive discussion of the forces which determined the distribution of immigrants in the years under review; we shall confine ourselves to an interesting attempt to organize an emigration company at Galesburg, Illinois.

The panic of 1857 left a trail of agricultural and industrial depression in the west, and Galesburg, with a population of some six or seven thousand of which about one thousand were Swedes, was hit particularly hard. Reverend T. N. Hasselquist, the pastor of the Swedish Lutheran church, wrote to *Hemlandet* stating conditions and requesting ministers and others to furnish information about prospects for settlement elsewhere, opportunities to pre-empt land, outlook for work, and anything pertinent.[32]

The response was gratifying, and on February 28, 1859, a meeting was held at which letters from Tennessee, Iowa, and Minnesota were read and the matter of moving discussed.[33] The long winters in Minnesota and the consequent necessity of feeding cattle in the stable from five to seven months and the numerous and "envise" mosquitoes were not sufficient to dissuade the majority from moving there or to northern Iowa. Nothing definite was decided, however, because no concerted movement could be undertaken that spring. It was decided to hold another meeting the following April.

This meeting was unusually well attended. Oscar Malmborg, from the land department of the Illinois Central railroad, was present and strongly presented the advantages

---

32) *Hemlandet,* January 13, 1859.
33) Letter from Hasselquist, in *Hemlandet,* March 8, 1859.

of Illinois. He said that Chicago being the market of the west, to settle far from that point, especially across the Mississippi, was to lessen income through higher freight rates; that it was good economy to pay more for Illinois land than for Iowa, Kansas, and Minnesota farms. As a further inducement he was authorized to state that no taxes would be levied on Illinois Central land until seven years after payment. The central Illinois climate is milder and more even, feed for cattle easier to procure, and schools and the comforts of life more accessible. Hasselquist wrote that many favored purchasing Illinois Central land. No decision was reached, however, but two men were appointed to inspect possible locations with instructions to view tile railway lands first.[34]

One of the representatives, J. C. Brandt, made a report of his tour through *Hemlandet*.[35] He was unable to travel widely in Minnesota because of lack of funds, but he visited Forest City, Hutchinson, Glencoe, and Scandian Grove, which places he describes concisely and well. On the whole he gained a most favorable impression of Minnesota.

Apparently the attempt to direct emigration on a large scale failed, but the meetings, discussions, and letters advertised certain communities and influenced decisions of individuals. Minnesota especially received a great deal of free advertising. Reverend P.A. Cederstam wrote from St. Peter as follows:[36] "Minnesota is now and is destined to become an important place for our Swedish Lutheran church, and a residence of four years has

---

[34] Letter from Oscar Malmborg, in *Hemlandet*, April 4, 1859; Hasselquist wrote an account of tile meeting, in *Hemlandet*, April 19, 1859.

[35] *Hemlandet*, August 10, 1859.

[36] *Hemlandet*, April 12, 1859.

thoroughly convinced me that no other state in the whole union will be so thickly populated with Swedes and their descendants as Minnesota." People who judged Minnesota by the rocky hills along the Mississippi to St. Paul, or up the Minnesota to Carver, or up the St. Croix to Stillwater, and pronounced the state a "humbug," were not acquainted with the real Minnesota. He urged the Galesburg Swedes to consider the following advantages of Minnesota: a climate like that of Sweden and the most healthful in the United States; plenty of good land; an already considerable Swedish population; concentration in a single state would insure the maintenance of Swedish churches and schools.

Louis Lybecker, of St. Louis, Missouri, who had heard of the Galesburg movement, was most enthusiastic about Minnesota.[37] "My knowledge about Kansas," he wrote, "is such that from the bottom of my heart I never want to think of it. What is a home for us *Nordboer* without summer, without snow, without woods and water? Are we used to an endless prairie with its eternal monotony? No; we feel at home when we find ourselves surrounded by a *herrlig* nature, of evergreen forests along a lake or river. Then we can say 'New Sweden.' Let us found a colony in southwestern Minnesota, or near our countrymen in that state. Let us not forget the north. I have never been in Minnesota, but it seems to me it is the right place for Swedes. Within a few years the road to Oregon without doubt will take its beginning in Minnesota.'[38]

---

37) *Hemlandet,* March 15, 1859.

38) In 1859 Dr. C. H. Cran of Andover, Illinois, attempted to organize a colony in Kansas. His "Kansas" meeting In Galesburg in 1857 was well attended and many Swedes were interested in his proposition, but his efforts ended in failure, as the reappearance of his medical advertisement in *Hemlandet* in December, 1859, bears witness. His idea was to operate on a communistic basis for a time. See *Hemlandet,* June 3, September 18, and December 3, 1857, and May 22 and December 18, 1858.

PILGRIM AND STRANGER

The Chronicles of
GEORGE M. STEPHENSON

I
AMERICA FEVER

[Peter Cassel] wielded a pen that vied with Marco Polo's.

One hundred years ago the inhabitants of Sweden became infected with a disease which came to be known as "America fever." The fever found its victims among those who were not inoculated with the virus of social distinction and economic prosperity; and it was transmitted by letters that found their way from America to the small red cottages among pine-clad, rocky hills. These letters made a tremendous impression on certain persons at a time when a new and ideal world was dawning in literature and in the press. They were read and pondered by the simple and credulous individuals to whom they were addressed; they were discussed in homes and at markets and fairs and churches; they were broadcast through the newspapers. The contents of these documents from another world were so thrilling and fabulous that the most fanciful stories were circulated about the land of milk and honey across the Atlantic.

It was reported that a wandering beggar girl painted America in even more attractive colors than Joshua's spies portrayed the promised land to the children of Israel. "In America," the girl said, "the hogs eat their fill of raisins and dates that everywhere grow wild; and when they are thirsty they drink from ditches flowing with wine."

One cannot escape the suspicion that the beggar girl had heard about a letter written at Jefferson County, Iowa, by a man from her parish, who in May 1845, had set sail from Gothenburg in search of a better life in the Western

Republic. The departure of this man in his fifty-sixth year at the head of a company of emigrants created a sensation in his parish and in neighboring parishes; and information about his adventure was eagerly awaited by his friends and relatives. They were not disappointed. Without the educational advantages enjoyed by the so-called "better folk" he wielded a pen that vied with Marco Polo's. Iowa's corn, pumpkins, and hogs, through the medium of his letter appeared as monstrous to the peasants in Sweden letter as Gulliver appeared to the inhabitants of Lilliput; and in contrast with the earnings of the American farmer, the income of the Swedish husbandman shrank to insignificance. Even the thunder in Sweden sounded like the report of a toy pistol, compared with the heavy artillery of the heavens in America.

The emigrant was not only impressed with America's rich soil, its forests, its abundance of coal and metals, its rivers and lakes swarming with fish, but he found himself elevated to a new world, where his former ideas of a society conforming more closely to nature's laws were suddenly made real, and he enjoyed a satisfaction in life that he had never before experienced. There were no beggars to remind him of the misery and poverty in Sweden; he had never heard of theft in the community; and he had yet to see a lock on a door in his neighborhood. The absence of class distinctions was indicated by the fundamental principles of the Constitution of the United States. He did not have to bare his head in the presence of counts, barons, and lords, for there were none. There were no large estates, whose owners took the last sheaf from their tenants.

From Sweden to America

Among the pilgrims who yearned for the Utopia on the American frontier was a farmer in Småland, whose name was Stephan. He was in the same situation as were the great majority of the peasant population of Sweden: he had no surname. His father's name was Stephan, and, following the custom of the country, he was known as Stephan Stephansson. Physically, he towered above his fellows; and only one man in the parish could measure his gigantic strength with his own.

Stephan knew of the emigrant in Jefferson County-Peter Cassel by name. In fact, he was probably acquainted with him, because for a time he had rented a farm in the parish from which he had emigrated. He had read his letter, or at least had first-hand information of its contents. The letter gave assurance that an emigrant possessed of a certain sum of money and endowed with hardihood could undertake the journey to America with confidence in a bright future for himself and his children. Indeed, it held out the promise that if his countrymen would notify the writer in advance of the approximate time of their arrival in New York, he would arrange to have one of his number meet them in New York and to guide them to their future home in Iowa. Pioneering in Iowa was not a serious challenge to a man whose superhuman strength was a byword in the parish; but no letter could convey to a Swedish peasant the vast distances of the Western Republic. Iowa could be no farther from New York than Stockholm was from Småland.

The new day dawned for Stephan and his wife and eight children—the eldest sixteen and the youngest two—when the rector of Södra Vi parish, on March 6, 1849, handed him a permit to emigrate from the kingdom of Oscar I—but not without preaching a sermon on the iniquity of violating the will of God by deserting the land of his birth. The letter of dismission certified that Stephan and his wife possessed approved knowledge of the fundamentals of Christianity and understood the doctrine of salvation in its simplicity; that they had communed at the Lord's Table on February 25; that they regularly attended catechetical meetings; that their conduct was blameless;

that Stephan had had smallpox and that his wife had been vaccinated; that they were not bound to service; and that they were enrolled on the tax lists for the year. The children had been vaccinated, and all but the three youngest were able to read. Only the eldest had been confirmed.

When Stephen humbly petitioned that the next to the oldest son, who was in his fourteenth year and had been instructed in the fundamentals of the Lutheran faith preparatory to confirmation, be confirmed by special arrangement, the request was peremptorily refused, and the refusal was emphasized by the admonition not to mock the All Highest by migrating to a country where neither God nor man was respected.

Stephen and his family were members of a company of emigrants numbering about two hundred who set sail from Gothenburg on May 19, 1849. After seven weeks and four days, New York was sighted. The journey up the Hudson River, through the Erie Canal and the Great Lakes, proceeded without serious incident; but at Chicago, which had already become the clearinghouse of immigration, the deadly cholera struck. The scourge was nationwide; and the President of the United States by proclamation set aside the first Friday in August as a day of fasting and prayer.

On the Illinois Canal, between Chicago and Peru, Stephan's four-year-old daughter was buried in a watery grave. The tragedy of lowering the coffin of rough boards into a grave filled with water on the bank of the canal was softened momentarily by the womenfolk who strewed wild flowers on the surface. Regulations did not permit the emigrants to enter the town of Peru; they were compelled to camp in the intense heat of the open prairie, while awaiting teamsters to take them on the overland journey.

From Peru to Andover, some thirty miles from Rock Island on the Mississippi, the sick were laid in wagons, baggage was tied onto the vehicles, and the able-bodied walked. When the caravan stopped to feed and water the horses, the sick were given attention and the dead were buried. Old and young were so exhausted that they were scarcely able to walk.

Upon arrival at the incipient Swedish settlement at Andover, Stephan learned of the tragic fate of countrymen who had preceded him. He saw the homeless, the sick, and the bewildered. Fathers and mothers had found an untimely end to their pilgrimages. There were neither crosses nor tombstones to mark their early graves.

Stephen found a temporary shelter for his family. After he had recovered from the effects of his experiences, he set out to view the land, which he found good and endless in extent. He saw many abandoned farms, whose owners had made arrangements with their erstwhile neighbors to sell them. The pale and emaciated appearance of his countrymen who had already established homes in the locality, together with his own experience in narrowly being cheated out of his savings, brought the decision to search elsewhere for a farm.

A chance meeting with a countryman who had settled in Jefferson County, Iowa, and who informed him that the Swedes in that community were in good health, determined the locality of Stephan's new home. The journey continued overland to Rock Island, down the Mississippi to Burlington, Iowa, and thence overland to the New Sweden settlement in Jefferson County, where the writer of the "America letter" had struck it rich.

For several days Stephan and his family enjoyed the hospitality of their countrymen, who were also of service in finding a farm. The land was hilly and overgrown with brush and thickets and oak, maple, hickory, linden, elm, and walnut trees. In common with the early emigrants from Sweden, Stephan wanted a farm where timber and water were near at hand. Moreover, they believed the soil of wooded land to be superior to the treeless prairies. Stephan purchased for $250.00 an eighty-acre farm, of which eleven acres were under cultivation and fenced, situated less than a half-mile from the Skunk River.

Stephan's experiences on the journey from Gothenburg to New Sweden and his reaction to his adopted country were related simply and graphically to his relatives and friends in Sweden in a long letter dated October 9, 1849, three months after his arrival in New York. The tragic events were not suppressed; but he waxed enthusiastic over the prospect of a better home in spiritual as well as material matters. There were no laws to restrict freedom of conscience. In Andover and in New Sweden he found ministers who were well versed in the Bible and in the correct interpretation. Unlike Sweden, where the sheep sought the shepherd and addressed him with high-sounding titles, in America the shepherd sought out the sheep. He mentioned the incident when, shortly before his departure, he was snubbed and lectured by the rector of his own parish. He wrote that the Americans were in all matters of conduct so strict that adultery, theft, and drunkenness were abhorred, and offenders were exposed and compelled to leave the neighborhood.

Elderly people were admonished to remain in the land of their fathers because, after the hardships of the journey, their best days would be over; but young folks who had fifty dollars in cash and provisions for fourteen weeks were assured of a glorious future. In America wages were so high that within four or five years they could save enough money to purchase land for themselves.

The sequel to this letter was written on May 17, 1854, exactly two days less than five years after Stephan set sail from Gothenburg. He was still happy that he had migrated to the land of liberty and had thereby delivered his children from the slavish drudgery that had been his lot. It must have been a great surprise to his readers to learn that if a laborer could not get along with his employer, he could leave his job at any time, and the employer was obliged to pay him for the time he had put in at the scale of wages that had been agreed upon for the month or year. Equally sensational was the information that he was free to move at any time and to any place without a certificate from an employer or from the parish pastor, because neither passports nor certificates were required as they were in Sweden. There was no class distinction, unlike Sweden where working people were looked dawn upon and called "rabble" in contrast with lazy gentlemen who were called 'better folk.'

In America labor was so well paid that in order to live a life of leisure, a man had to be in possession of great wealth. The man of toil did not have to be satisfied with black bread. White bread was on the daily menu, and coffee and tea took the place of gruel. The country took pity on widows and orphans, who were supplied with food and clothing by the county. For the drunkard, however, there was no mercy. Alcohol was used sparingly and mostly for medicinal purposes. Stephan detected a great difference between the moral standards in the United States and in Sweden. Even the "heathen" measured up to Christian standards of conduct, he wrote.

Within three years after Stephen had written this optimistic letter, he and all but three members of his family were stricken by the deadly typhus that attacked families who lived on the bottom lands of the Skunk River which overflowed its banks in the spring. The mournful events were recorded on simple markers in the Lutheran cemetery in New Sweden. Stephen died at the age of forty-eight in April 1855. His widow and two sons died in March 1857. The youngest member of the family, a daughter of ten years, passed away in the following month; and her lifeless body lay in the pioneer home on the day of the auction sale to liquidate the personal estate of her father.

Stephan's span of life was short. Fate deprived him and most of his family of America's blessings; but he left a goodly heritage to a son and two daughters. His circle of friends and acquaintances extended to pioneers whose forbears felled the forest and tilled the soil of New England, New York, Pennsylvania, Ohio, Indiana, and

Illinois. His own name and the names of his wife and children speedily became Americanized. He became known as "Stephen Stephenson" and "Steven Stevenson"; and his wife's name was changed from Christina Cathrina to "Christina Catherine." Paulus became "Paul"; Olaus became "Oliver"; Carl Johan became "Charles John"; Anna Cathrina became "Anna Caroline"; Ingrid Stina became "Ingrid Christine"; and Maria became "Mary."

Oliver Stephenson, Survivor

Stephan's mantle fell on his only surviving son, Olaus, whose Americanized name had already become Oliver Stephenson. As a boy of fourteen he had experienced the hardships and the sorrow of the journey from Gothenburg to Jefferson County. In his letter of 1854 Stephen proudly related that Oliver was earning thirteen dollars a month as a "hired hand." He inherited the large frame and unusual strength of his father; but at the time of the auction sale, he was so crippled with rheumatism, and so helpless, that he overheard people remark that it would have been better if he had died instead of his able-bodied brothers.

About a half-mile from the homestead of the late Stephen, there lived an old woman who was known as "Granny Dutch." She was reputed to have worked miraculous cures by "rubbing" and by mumbling unintelligible words. Some days after the sale Oliver, unobserved, crawled on hands and knees to the cabin of "Granny Dutch," who said she could cure him. Whether the miracle was worked by the old woman's skillful hands, or by the hocus pocus of words, or by the effort to crawl to her cabin-the reader may decide. The fact is that within a few days Oliver was walking, and within months he was discharging the duties of a porter in a hotel in Mount Pleasant, the county seat of Henry County which was adjacent to Jefferson county.

With the aid of parish records and personal correspondence we are able to trace the inception of another family migration from Småland to Iowa and also the inception of a romance in the lives of Oliver and Mary Stephenson.

Oliver Marries Mary Helena

No parish in Småland was immune to "America fever." On May 11, 1858, a farmer in the parish of Edshult, not far from Jönköping, took out a permit to emigrate for five men and two women. In the company of this family was a girl of twenty years, Mary Helena, a niece of the farmer, who left her parents and three sisters and a brother. Mary accompanied her relatives to Jefferson County; but within a short time she was writing letters from Mount Pleasant, where she was employed as a housemaid. Heartaches, tragedy, joy, and romance were texts of her simple, poorly spelled letters, which were stained with tears.

Mary bade her parents not to worry about her. She told them that she had fared well in Sweden and expected to fare even better in America. With a letter dated May 7, 1859, she enclosed a daguerreotype of herself and another picture which she was certain would be welcome, because it was the likeness of a man who is to become your second son-in-law sometime this fall." She apologized for the haste with which the second picture was sent; but it was entrusted to the care of a man who was returning to Sweden to claim his inheritance. Mary explained that her "intended" was an emigrant from Södra Vi parish, who had been in the country for ten years; and she added "one who has been here that length of time is acquainted with the language and customs of the country."

Oliver and Mary Stephenson were married on February 2, 1860, and began housekeeping on a farm, which had been purchased the year before. Mary kept her parents informed of the prosperity and welfare of her husband and herself; but the longing for parents and sisters and brother could not be suppressed. In several letters the hope was expressed that they would become infected with "America fever."

Moreover, these years were darkened by the heavy clouds of war and the fate of the Republic appeared to hang in the balance. Five months after the battle of Gettysburg, Oliver wrote that it was the greatest war the world had ever known. Thousands fell in battle almost every day; but he doubted that the South could hold out much longer. Land was cheap, partly because of the number of men in the army and partly because many were taking up unimproved land, where farms were free, thanks to the approval of the Homestead Act by President Lincoln. Mary wrote that it was noticeable that the side reserved for men in church was sparsely occupied. At gatherings of young people, girls outnumbered the men five or six to one.

Without exception, the letters expressed satisfaction end pride in the adopted country and gratitude for the home it had given them. Oliver wrote about his increasing livestock--horses, cattle, oxen, mules, calves, hogs, and chickens; about bountiful crops; and about relatives and acquaintances from Edshult parish. Some of them had gone to the gold fields in Idaho Territory, where work was back-breaking, wages were fabulous, and living costs were in proportion. One gold-seeker had returned with four thousand dollars in gold; and his brother-in-law, who was married to his younger sister, had earned six dollars a day by making wheelbarrows for the fortune hunters.

Mary's letters were saddened by bnging for loved one's in Sweden and were redolent of the pietism of Bunyan's *Pilgrim's Progress*, a Swedish translation of which was her lifelong companion. She wrote of dreaming about Sweden, especially in anticipation of a letter; but the only thing that could induce her to return to her native land was the pleasure of being with her relatives. She wrote that

Americans lived much better than people in Sweden, and they were not wanting in spiritual food. She spread a much better table than housewives in the old country: wheat bread, beef, pork, eggs, syrup, apples, cherries. Not only did she weave clothing for Oliver, but she also augmented their income by selling cloth to her neighbor for two dollars a yard. Although the distance to the Swedish church was great, they were privileged to hear the preaching of the Word of God by an itinerant minister, who was a better shepherd than many pastors in Sweden. On Sundays when the minister was absent, the faithful gathered to hear the reading of sermons by a layman who could measure his ability with parish pastors. But there were always the lingering memories of the parental home and Sweden's healthful climate.

"By the grace of God we are prospering and laying up a little each year. For this we have God alone to thank," wrote Oliver in 1864. He had sold his farm and had purchased another in the same community; but he was restless and even thought of selling out and undertaking a voyage to Sweden, in order to satisfy Mary's longing for her parents and to appraise with more mature judgment the relative advantages of America and Sweden. But fate ordained that neither Oliver nor Mary was to share the experiences of many returned emigrants who thought of Sweden in terms of the parish church, the red cottage, the lakes, confirmation mates, and parents, only to learn that within a few years America had worked her magic. The language they spoke was a jargon of English and Swedish dialect, with many words unintelligible to old friends; Sweden was a country of scanty wages, brutal employers, high titles, and a gloomy future; in America there were no privileged classes—no scorn for the man of toil.

Although they perhaps did not realize it at the time, Oliver and Mary had already taken root. Their family had increased. They liked and admired their friendly neighbors who estimated their fellow men in terms of industry, integrity, and self-respect. There was a spirit of give-and-take, which made for easy social intercourse and business transactions. Like thousands of their countrymen, Oliver and Mary rose to the dignity of American citizenship without a fine pedigree. With only thirteen days of schooling to his credit in Sweden, Oliver wrote both English and Swedish. With no schooling at all, Mary wrote long Swedish letters, but her use of spoken and written English was limited. Oliver was a man of affairs who even learned to speak German to his German neighbors; and in later years it was an exciting and amusing time for their children when old acquaintances from Jefferson County spent a few days with Oliver and Mary in their newer home in the adjacent Henry County. The children were no less impressed by their father's versatility when he conversed in German with Jewish peddlers, who not infrequently asked for the privilege of lodging for the night.

II
A NEW HOME IN SWEDESBURG

*I think of Swedesburg as a home
from which I have never been absent*

In 1865 the Jefferson County farm was sold. Then, if ever, the voyage to Sweden ought to have been undertaken; but Oliver was not enthusiastic, and Mary yielded to his judgment. In Henry County, a three-hours' drive from the Skunk River, Oliver purchased a farm of 160 acres of rolling prairie land for the sum of $4,500. A few Swedes had already settled on land farther east in the same township, where the swampy land was overgrown with marsh grass and was, in the opinion of many, "good only for ducks and Swedes." It remained good for ducks and furnished a scanty living for Swedes until terra-cotta tile ended for all time crop failures in wet years.

In the course of years, Oliver's farm was improved by tiling; but in the meantime the rolling prairie yielded ample crops of corn, oats, rye, wheat, buckwheat, sugar cane, and timothy. There were apple, plum, cherry, and peach trees; raspberry, gooseberry, and current bushes; grapevines, strawberry beds; a bountiful garden; and shade trees and groves for windbreaks. The livestock included cattle, horses, sheep, and hogs, and there were barns and sheds to shelter them. There were chickens by the hundreds, and their chorus was augmented by turkeys, ducks, guineas, and peacocks.

The original farm was extended to include a half-section by the purchase of adjoining farms. The original dwelling was displaced by a ten-room house. The "old house" was used as a summer kitchen. There was a smokehouse for curing meat, a milkhouse, a canepress, a cidermill, a granary, several corncribs, a toolhouse, sheds to protect implements, wagons, buggies, and a carriage.

Stephenson Family Home
c. 1880

The home in Wayne Township, Henry County, was a clearinghouse for immigrants: a miniature immigration depot. It happened on one occasion that Oliver and Mary and their children were surprised to see several wagons drive onto the premises. There were some forty persons in the party, with trunks, satchels, parcels, and bundles. These immigrants had by mistake been put off a train at a station of the Chicago Rock Island, and Pacific Railway, twenty or more miles distant. One or more members of the party knew of Oliver and his post office address. There were few, if any, Swedes residing in the town; but inquiries yielded the necessary information, with the result that the bewildered immigrants were somehow lodged and fed until they boarded a Chicago, Burlington, and Quincy Railroad train which took them to their destination.

In this case "America Letters" brought uninvited guests; but Oliver and Mary's letters attracted others who were rewarded with a share in the bounties of the Mississippi Valley. "According to reports, conditions in Sweden must be very unfortunate for the poor and the great majority of the people," wrote Oliver in 1867. "I believe they would do better to come to America." In a postscript Mary added that according to indications, about half the population of Sweden would come to America that spring. She also wrote about the arrival of seventeen emigrants from Nydala parish. "We housed and fed them, because they had no relatives or acquaintances. One family is still with us. People are arriving in large numbers from Sweden and other countries and sections; but do not worry about the danger of overpopulation, because Iowa is as large as Sweden and only half settled. Then think of the other states."

Again and again the refrain was sounded that parents would do well by their children to make the sacrifice of migrating to America. Mary knew of persons who owned farms who didn't even have gruel in Sweden.

One immigrant whose possessions on arrival consisted only of his clothing after a few years had enough money to buy a good estate in Sweden. "This in spite of" the fact that he married a poor girl, suffered misfortunes, and had no one to help him. But he has an industrious and good wife."

That many homes in Sweden were scenes of lively and prayerful debates before the decision to emigrate was reached is illustrated by the correspondence that passed between Mary and her parents. Mary assured them that they would not be obliged to live with them and to endure the annoyances of her children. They could have a home of their own. They were not expected to drudge for her family. "I will soon have help with the housework; and, as Oliver employs a hand in the fall and during the summer, he doesn't need assistance. We are not in the habit of taking things easy, although it would not be necessary to work so hard. However, for one in good health and brought up to hard work, there is no hardship connected with it.

If you would like to live with us, you will find a hearty welcome from both of us. We will take care of you in your old age—God only knows if that day will ever dawn. My eyes are filled with tears as I write about it."

Mary hoped that one of her sisters would accompany her parents. Lest the worry of traveling alone might weigh too heavily, Oliver offered to make the trip to Sweden. He urged his brothers-in-law to use their savings to pay their passage to America. If perchance they were in need of financial assistance, Oliver would pay their passage. Mary's father was early persuaded by her fervent letters; but her mother was reluctant. This brought the admonition that under no circumstances should they separate. Weigh the matter carefully," Mary wrote. "I am sorry for Mother if she is persuaded to go against her will."

In January 1869, Mary's anxiety was relieved. She wrote that she was happy to learn that her parents intended to come; but the event was so far in the future that she could not "bide the time." "We are of the opinion that, having made the decision, you ought to come as soon as possible.... Perhaps you will be ready sooner than you think." Her letter, and Oliver's which accompanied it, gave instructions about taking along provisions and warned against "rascals who make it a business to cheat the immigrants."

The final chapter was a letter from Oliver, dated February 5, 1869: "I bid you a hearty welcome to this free country. Immediately on your arrival in New York, notify me of the time of your arrival at Mount Pleasant, so that I can meet you." Mary added a postscript: "Thanks for the good news that we shall soon see you. I believe that God has directed this, because it has always been next to my heart. I have thought and dreamed of this constantly."

On April 11, 1869, emigration permits were issued to Mary's parents and to her sister and brother-in-law.

III
A BOY'S LIFE ON THE FAMILY FARM

I felt that I had come to the state of manhood when at the age of eight I "drove the hayfork" with Old Fanny, the gentlest horse on the place.

I have a clear picture of my childhood world, whose capital city was the farmstead; but I do not have the faintest idea when I became conscious that I was a resident of Wayne Township, Henry County, Iowa, and that Iowa was one of the United States of America. I do recall that I asked my Father who owned the road that brought us to the Swedish Lutheran Church at Swedesburg. When he replied that it belonged to Uncle Sam, I wondered what he looked like and where he lived. Uncle Sam was almost as mysterious as God, whom I associated with the thunder that rumbled in the distance. I associated thunder with the fanningmill that stood in the barn. When I struck the metal drum of this machine, it made the loudest noise-- next to thunder--that I had ever heard. I wondered what need God had of so many fanningmills.

My family left the farm before I was old enough to experience the drudgery and hard work that fell to the lot of my brothers and sisters. My sister whose daily duty was to "hunt eggs" bribed me to deal with cross hens who refused to leave their nests, by praising my courage; and at the age of six or seven my "chore" was to fill the woodbox in the kitchen and to bring in baskets of corncobs which were used for fuel. Occasionally I had the duty of turning the grindstone and of operating the churn. Although I had reached the age of nine before leaving the farm, for some reason I was not required to "cover corn" -- hills which the cornplanter had missed. My Father was generous enough to suggest that I run the chaff from the hay that accumulated on the floor of the barn through the fanningmill and paid me for each half-bushel of timothy seed.

Being the youngest of nine children, I received the attention and favors that were usually bestowed on the "baby." I wore better clothing and had more toys and playthings, including a wagon, which was the envy of visiting children because it was unique in the neighborhood, a popgun, which was almost as sensational, and games like "lotto," "tiddlywinks," and "authors." I never saw a deck of playing cards, and I am sure that Oliver and Mary never saw one in their home. Their children were inoculated against playing cards by hearing stories about the dire fate of persons in Sweden who had been tempted of the devil and had met the fate of his disciples.

My brothers were too old to indulge in my childish interests. A sister was my only playmate, and our interests did not coincide, except when we played games. The buildings on the farm represented my knowledge of geography. A corncrib was Morning Sun, a town I had heard Oliver speak about; a cattlebarn was Wayland, a town six miles to the west which I had never seen, and so on. Almost every tree had a name; and I can still name in order the eight maple trees that shaded the barnyard. I can still see them sway before the storms that rolled up from the northwest. I can still hear the ever increasing volume of thunder and see the ominous flashes of lightning from the angry thunderhead that was partly hidden by the barn as I looked out the kitchen window and watched the weathervane on the cupola. The unusual activity of the pigeons that made their home in the cupola, and the inevitable turning of the weathervane, told me that the storm was about to break.

Mary was always anxious about the men in the field. She scanned the horizon in the direction of the field where the plow or the seeder or the mower was in action, and. wondered why Oliver and the boys didn't leave their work sooner. But Oliver was economical in the use of time, as he was in the use of everything else. Many years after he had left the farm, I was told that his reputation in the community was that he never got tired and that at threshing time it was considered a cruel punishment to be assigned to work alongside of him.

My naming of objects on the farm extended also to the livestock. Some names were fictitious, end others were suggested by individuals in the community. An impressive-looking rooster, who walked with a slight limp, was given the name of a veteran of the Civil War; and a venerable hen reminded me of a character in the *Chatterbox*. It goes without saying that the horses and cows were named—usually not by me—but for some reason the hogs were ignored. I singled out a few sheep for special distinction. Every year a carload or two of steers were fattened for market; but except for one or two in each herd that bore some distinguishing mark, or were hard to manage, they were nameless. A bull was named "Hendricks" in honor of a Vice President, but it was a dubious honor, conferred as it was by a family so strongly Republican as ours.

Oliver was a stern, exacting, and sometimes unreasonable man who demanded the best from his family and hired help; but his exactness and insistence on system and order were based on fundamental justice and charity. He had no patience with idlers and wasters; but no worthy man or woman was turned away from his door, nor did he refuse a loan of money to anybody whose industry and fidelity to duty had been demonstrated. I have heard testimony from men who approached him for a loan, and were surprised to have him inquire if the amount was sufficient and astonished when informed that no note was required. That may have been good psychology, because some of the debtors informed me that they took a solemn vow to pay that loan above all others.

Likewise, Oliver's care for his livestock may have been hardheaded economy, rather then sentiment, because he bestowed the same careful husbanding upon his implements and machinery. Horses that worked all week were rested on the Sabbath. Cattle, horses, and hogs were provided with protection from wind and cold; and in the winter it was somebody's job to prevent foolish chickens from roosting in trees in the orchard.

One cold morning Oliver brought into the kitchen a lamb whose chances for life were dubious. I was told that if she lived and if I took care of her, she would be mine. With the assistance of my sisters, a warm place was prepared for her in the summer kitchen; and day-by-day I watched the process of feeding until she was able to stand. Within a day or two her bleating assured us that my property was safe. To my great disappointment, it was proposed that the lamb be returned to her dam; but my pet was entirely weaned and to the end of her days would have nothing to do with sheep. She was a privileged character and insisted that she be treated as a member of the family. A pen was built especially for her in a corner of the sheephouse; and it was my privilege to escort her to it after the sheep had been shut up for the night. During the day she had the run of the farm; and there was scarcely a fence or a gate that defied her ingenuity. She invariably responded with a bleat when her name was called and understood what was said to her. If sheep are stupid, my understudy was the exception that proves the rule.

Our farm was in a sense an economic unit. Except for clothing, boots, shoes, furniture, vehicles, implements, tools, sugar, coffee, spices, and certain other commodities, the necessities of life were produced on the farm. Mary carded wool, made the spinning wheel hum, wove carpets, made soap, smoked meat, prepared rennet, churned butter, made cheese, moulded candles, sewed garments for members of the family, fed chickens and calves, gave her children first lessons in reading, gave assistance to neighbors, and attended to the thousand and one duties that fell to the lot of a mother of nine children.

Except for the Sabbath, which was kept holy, there were few idle days. On rainy days when outdoor work was interrupted, the boys and the hired men were set to work running grain through the fanningmill, greasing and repairing wagons, buggies, implements, and harness, while Oliver performed the more exacting repair work, even to half-soling shoes for young and old. In lieu of other jobs there was always carpentry, cleaning and rearranging the barn, cellar, or toolhouse, sorting potatoes and apples, repairing fences, and the like. During the winter months work was less pressing, but there was always the livestock to feed and water,

Oliver's economy of time took little account of recreation and amusement. He often spoke of improving one's time. There was virtue in hard work; there was evil in idleness and play, which was perhaps the philosophy of the man who had come up the hard way. It was only on rare occasions that his children asked him for money; and they stood a better chance of a favorable response if the request was for a quarter, or a half-dollar, or a dollar, instead of a nickel or a dime, because only candy could be purchased for the smaller amount, whereas something worthwhile might be procured for a larger coin. Not infrequently did he surprise us by handing us a silver dollar, or even a five-dollar bill, usually with the admonition to use it wisely or to keep it for a later time.

He was an expert in the use of the pocketknife and the ax; and it sometimes happened that when he observed us clumsily attempting to make a windmill or some other article, he interrupted his work and turned out a product that delighted us. In order encourage thrift and to inculcate a sense of responsibility, certain rows of corn were assigned to the boys, with the understanding that they might have the proceeds from the sale of the harvest if they husbanded it with care. The girls might be given a pig or a calf under the same system of reward for faithful work.

Fieldwork was exclusively the occupation of men, except during harvest, when one of the older girls was drafted to load hay to alleviate a labor shortage. During the hot days of harvest, the womenfolk brought cold water, and sometimes coffee and cookies and cake, to the men in the field. There was always a jug of water concealed under a shock of oats or rye to protect it from the rays of the sun. During seeding and cornplanting and harvest there was an hour of noon rest; and this interval was no less for the benefit of the horses.

Oliver always stacked his grain—unlike a few neighbors who threshed from shock—which meant that his threshing was delayed until the first part of September. It seemed to me that our stacks of grain were higher and more numerous than the stacks on neighboring farms, but I may have been mistaken. I do remember that our threshing lasted three or four days—unless rain intervened—and that our straw pile was larger and higher. Some years the threshing rig, as it was called, was moved to the "other place," which we called the second farm that was incorporated into the farmstead.

The preliminaries to threshing brought arduous duties to the womenfolk, who made preparation for serving two meals a day to a "gang" that filled two long tables. Perhaps my taste for mutton dates back to threshing time, when, in order to provide fresh meat, two sheep were butchered. It was a novelty and a treat to have fresh meat during the summer. Rarely did a "meat peddler" ply his trade in our community. More often did fish peddlers appear. Sometimes Oliver would strike a bargain and buy the entire stock of carp and catfish. Returning to threshing, in addition to mutton the "hands" ate their fill of chicken and a wide variety of victuals that every housewife in our community could prepare.

Once I accompanied Oliver on his mission to recruit threshing hands. As I remember it, his first question after driving into the barnyard was: "Do you want to swap thrashing this year, Henry?" If the reply was affirmative, it was next in order to state the approximate time of the threshing, the number of hands to be furnished, the number of teams of horses, and the like.

It was a thrilling moment for me when in the distance I heard the approach of the steam traction engine. The height of excitement came when the strange machine turned into the barnyard gate, followed by the water tank, the separator, and a wagon or two. I watched the process of planking the culvert that spanned the slough, the puffing of *the* engine as it was maneuvered into position, the setting of the separator, and the connecting of engine and separator by means of a long belt. In those days, before the straw-burner, the farmer furnished the coal or wood for the firebox, with enough fuel to move the outfit to the next farm.

I left the farm before the self-feeder and the wind-stacker became standard equipment on the separator; but I was too young to cut bands. I watched the skill with which the feeder avoided the sharp knives of the band-cutters, as he reached for the sheaves to feed them into the maw of the separator.

The main attraction was the traction engine. Perhaps the greatest thrill of my life on the farm was when the engineer lifted me to the platform and gave me a seat on the toolbox, where I could feel the throbbing of the engine; and I had something to tell the "folks" about after he had permitted me to blow the whistle. I can still remember the name of the engineer, but my ambition to follow his vocation was not realized. Many years later a locomotive engineer invited me to ride in his cab; but even that thrilling experience did not rise to the heights of my experience with the traction engine.

Another highlight in my career as a farmer was hay harvesting time, when the hayfork was brought into action to hoist the new-mown hay into the mow. "Driving the hayfork" was an assignment that fell to the youngest boy;

and I felt that I had come to the state of manhood when at the age of eight I drove "Old Fanny," the gentlest horse on the place. The only difficult part of the job was to hold up the singletree on the return trip; but Oliver, who usually procured up-to-date implements, bought a newfangled singletree which relieved me of that and was easier on Fanny's heels.

In our home the molasses pitcher was conspicuous at almost every meal, as it probably was in the homes of our neighbors. Oliver made our own sorghum. In the early fall the stalks of cane fell victim to the cornknife, and I well remember the sharp stubble this instrument left, much more serious than corn stubble for the boy who stumbled and fell while trailing his brothers who were hunting rabbits and prairie chickens. Oliver's canepress was available, without charge, for neighbors from near and far, who drove up with loads of cane, just as his platform scale was common property.

It was a novel sight to see the canepress in use drawn by horses; but it was more fun to watch Oliver cook sorghum in a flat-bottomed boiler that was heated by wood or cobs in a brick furnace. After each batch of sorghum, the family and guests "licked the platter clean" with slices of fresh bread. Of the many good things that came from the larder, the warm sorghum and newly baked bread eaten in the dusk of the dying embers of the fire has priority in my memory. I do not remember how many barrels of sorghum were made every fall; but I do remember that at least one molasses barrel stood in the cellar alongside of barrels of cider, vinegar, soft soap, and salt, kegs of wine, hundreds of jars of fruit, jelly, and jam, apples, potatoes, pumpkins, carrots, and perhaps other vegetables that could stored for a time. Other products of the farm included a score or more of cheeses, potato starch, and hominy.

Interesting, exciting, and also terrifying to a boy was butchering, which came in the early winter, late enough to freeze meat that did not lend itself to salting and pickling. The whole family was busy on butchering day. Sometimes a neighbor who was especially skilled was employed to assist, but more often Oliver and Mary superintended the various jobs.

I have mentioned the activities and duties on the farm that have lingered in my memory. The people in the community were industrious and carried a high degree of self-respect, as attested by their well-kept farms, which were enclosed by hedge fences. It was not until the early years of the present century that barbed wire and woven wire fences displaced the troublesome hedges which had to be trimmed two or three times a year. "Trimming hedge" was a job on rainy days and when work was slack. Before Oliver left the farm, most of the snaky rail fences had been replaced by wire.

The treeless prairies were barren of fuel for cook stoves and heating stoves. Oliver was one of several farmers in Wayne Township who owned a tract of wooded land—five or ten acres—on the river bottoms. "Going to the timber" was an annual event in the fall. It was an all-day job to cut down trees, to load logs on wagons, and to haul them home. For some days axes, saws, and wedges were busy; and before cold weather set in the wood was piled within convenient distance from the house. Until we moved to the city, my experience with coal smoke was confined to infrequent trips to the nearest railroad station, four miles away, and to the county seat, twelve miles away, except for a trip by rail in my third or fourth year.

Our home was illuminated with kerosene lamps. There were hanging lamps in the sitting room and parlors but they were lighted only when "company came." The portable lamps were of various sizes. There were several candleholders within easy access, and it seemed to me that Oliver and Mary preferred to use them. A burning candle was a convenient device for lighting Oliver's pipe. Oliver's economy of matches even caused him to resort to the laborious method of lighting his pipe by fishing out a live ember from the stove by means of a poker or by igniting a stick of kindling.

Mary taught me an unexpected lesson in economy, which made a deep impression. She was working in the garden when I appeared eating a slice of bread. I threw the crust on the ground, whereupon Mary firmly grasped my arm and read a lecture on the sinfulness of wasting the gifts God had bestowed upon us. "Some day," she said, "you may be in such want that you will have to beg a crust of bread." Later in life I learned that in that part of Sweden from which Mary emigrated to throw away bread was a gross sin, a mockery of God.

A people forced to eke out a frugal existence on the stony and sterile soil of Småland, and reduced by periodic famines to the extremity of eating bark bread or bread made from rye which remained unripened by drought, accepted in humble gratitude the blessings and bounties of nature. Mary's parents, who arrived in America in 1869, had told her about the successive crop failures in the years 1867, 1868, and 1869, when the people of Småland were reduced to the verge of starvation. Nobody remembered such a drought. The lean cows roamed at large; houses and farms were deserted; and at railroad stations there were crowds begging for bread. In desperation those who were able stampeded to America, some of them abandoning farms and sacrificing whatever of value they owned.

Mary impressed on us the lesson that nobody really sacrificed anything by bestowing gifts of money, food, and clothing on the needy. They paid dividends in the present and in the future, she said. The alleviation of poverty and sorrow brought on by sickness and death was an obligation resting on every individual in the community. It was my privilege to accompany my sisters on errands of mercy to homes where mothers were laid low by prolonged illness, or where old age or misfortune brought tragedy and sorrow. We brought to these homes milk, butter, bread, meat, canned fruit, clothing, and sometimes money. Tramps were invited into the kitchen for a square meal; and if they came in the evening, they were given lodging. It happened on one occasion that an unusually "tough customer" who asked for lodging was locked up for the night in a downstairs bedroom, where he rested until Oliver released him when he arose for the day, which was generally five o'clock.

Mary taught her children to have compassion for the aged, the infirm, and the crippled. An attempt to imitate or to ridicule them brought stern reproof or a whipping that would guarantee no repetition of the offense. We were taught to have an attitude of reverence toward nature and not to mock the Creator by making light-hearted remarks about natural phenomena or by imitating the sound of thunder.

We were constantly reminded of the uncertainty of life. It was exasperating to a boy who inquired innocently about certain plans for the future to be told by his parents that there was no assurance that "we will live until next summer."

There was, however, a lighter side of life in which Mary and Oliver joined. They had a keen sense of humor and delighted in telling stories that presented the amusing and the ridiculous in human affairs. I have written that Oliver's economy of time took little account of recreation or amusement. It may be, however, that his economy of time and his idea of recreation were more wholesome than that of his children. On rare occasions when Barnum's and Ringling's three-ring circuses came to Mount Pleasant, it was generally convenient for all but the very youngest members of the family to arise with the sun, in order to set aside the day for shopping in the forenoon and for attending the performance in the big tent in the afternoon. Oliver was just as enthusiastic about the performers and just as interested in the menagerie as were other spectators.

In the autumn there were always teams and wagons ready for the annual outing to gather hazelnuts, hickory nuts, and walnuts. One or more members of the family were invited to accompany Oliver to the mill on the Skunk River; and while waiting for the grist to be ground, he instructed them in the art of luring catfish and carp.

IV
LEARNING AT HOME AND SCHOOL

The lark is up to meet the sun;
The bee is on the wing;
The ant his labor has begun.

My family was bilingual: both English and Swedish were spoken in our home. Oliver usually spoke English to us, except when he was angry or excited, and of course we spoke English to him. Although Mary had "worked out" in the home of an American family for a year or more before her marriage, she had been deprived of the wider contacts that Oliver had made and for that reason spoke English with difficulty and always conversed with her children in her native tongue. After I had learned to read, I sometimes asked her to read the captions of the pictures in the torn and frayed Chatterbox, which I still have in my possession. Her Swedish accent amused me, and I suspect that she exaggerated it because it brightened the life of her little boy. When I asked her if everybody would "become Swedes in heaven," she evaded the question. My recollection is that she left that problem to God. What prompted the question was probably the dilemma that faced other bilingual children. My religious instruction was in Swedish; my prayers, my devotional literature, and my Sunday school lessons were in Swedish, so much so that more than once when I was compelled to commit to memory Luther's Catechism I lamented that Jesus was a Swede.

Not until many years after I left the farm did I become conscious that the community where I was born was the United States of America in miniature. I was no more conscious of the processes of history than were millions of my countrymen who were actors in the drama of the nineteenth century. I did not know that I was one of the weavers of a unique fabric of society and that I was a member of a union whose membership was composed of men and women of all races and creeds. A few prophets had peered over the horizon into the twentieth century, but they saw through a glass darkly. At the time of the World's Colombian Exposition in Chicago in 1893, a prophetic historian, Frederick Jackson Turner, who many years later became my mentor in the graduate school, presented a paper which was a pioneer attempt to chart the course of the past and to suggest a chart for the future.

I accepted my bilingual fate without inquiring into the circumstances. It was no more strange or unusual than the sight of the Amish families who drove by in platform buggies. I never inquired why the Amish men wore clothes with hooks and eyes and why the women wore black sunbonnets in summer and black hoods in winter. I heard the expression, "The Dutch and the dog fennel will soon take this country," but it had no meaning to me.

In our family, as in other Swedish families, children were taught to speak Swedish before they learned the language of the country, and as a consequence when some of them entered the district school they understood English imperfectly and could not speak it. Within a few months, however, the school worked the miracle of converting the playground into a forum where English was the only medium of communication. As the youngest member of the family, I learned to speak and read English and Swedish simultaneously.

My formal and informal education began before I enrolled in the district school. My youngest sister, who was four years older than I, was appointed by Mary to teach me to read and spell in McGuffey's First Reader and soon I was able to repeat from memory "The lark is up to meet the sun; the bee is on the wing; the ant his labor has begun." A portion of the time for instruction was allotted to reading and spelling in a Swedish primer, in which my instructor was also proficient. At the age of four I was student of two languages.

Mary's pedagogical methods were excellent. A certain time each day was set aside for the lesson. Teacher and pupil were seated at the foot of the stairway that led from the dining room to the upper story. Mary was occupied in the kitchen, within hearing distance and on the alert to intervene should teacher and pupil fall into disagreement or divert attention from the business at hand. A time or two I detected that Mary saw the humorous aide of certain situations. After a few months of "primary" instruction, I was on my own; but there was always a member of the family available when assistance was needed.

Mary's discipline was severe-the lesson had to be learned-but the rewards were generous. I do not know when and where it originated, but I suspect that the reward of merit employed by Mary was imported from Sweden. After the lesson had been recited, the book was mysteriously laid away in a quiet end remote room, usually under a pillow. I was advised to play out of doors and admonished not to disturb the quiet of the room where the miracle was to be worked. After a few minutes, I was told that it was safe to enter the room; and invariably I found a piece of candy or a penny between the covers of the reader. My explanation of the miracle was simple: I gave the credit to the rooster whose image was printed on the last page of Swedish primer. My recollection is that McGuffey's First Reader was blessed with a similar illustration. The fowls were equally generous; but I did not understand why the crow of the Swedish rooster was "kuk-e-li-lu," and why the crow of the American brother was "cock-a-doodle-do."

Four months before I celebrated my sixth birthday I enrolled in the district school, which was kept in a typical Midwestern schoolhouse about three-quarters of a mile from our home. My two sisters next of age were my schoolmates. The older sister, who was my senior by eight years, took me under her wing and made arrangements for us to occupy the same desk—a customary procedure. The desk that was suitable for a pupil of her age was too high for me; but that detail concerned neither the teacher nor my parents. Moreover, the seat was in need of repair and was unnecessarily uncomfortable, but that detail concerned neither the teacher nor the school directors. My feet did not touch the floor, but that, too, was unimportant.

My sister was an exacting and sympathetic tutor. She was aware of the rivalry between older sisters and brothers to have the youngest members of their respective families excel in arithmetic and spelling. She saw to it that I was not negligent in preparing for those recitations, and made sure that I was among those who were awarded "headmarks" —citations for merit and good conduct. It was common knowledge that when a class in spelling stood in line before the school, and a pupil hesitated over a word, the lips of an older sister or brother were seen to form vowels and consonants.

The schoolhouse, judged by standards of the present day, was unattractive and poorly equipped. The blackboard, which was seldom used, was painted on the board wall at the front of the room. There were only two erasers— homemade contraptions of woolly sheepskin tacked on a block of wood—and a single chalk box, which was "spoken for" by a pupil long before it was empty. Lunch boxes— dinner pails, we called them—were placed on shelves that lined a wall; and a pail of water, with a dipper, stood on a chair. The water in the well in the schoolyard was foul, which made it necessary for two boys to "pack water" drawn from a well on an adjacent farm.

A wood stove stood in the center of the room. On cold mornings the children huddled around the red-hot stove and flue. One day my youngest sister and I were the only pupils in attendance. A snowstorm warned parents to keep their children at home but in our family absence from school was a major sin. All day the storm raged. In spite of it, the teacher "kept school" until four o'clock, which was the time for "school to let out." I don't know what became of the teacher; but I do know that after my sister and I had battled our way home and had related the extraordinary proceedings of the day, there was no comment within the family circle other than commendation because we were braver than our schoolmates. Upon reflection, I suspect that the teacher did not dismiss us because to have done so would have meant a reduction in her meager salary.

During the four years I attended this school, there were nine successive teachers: five women and four men. I thought the women were better teachers. It was customary to engage men for the winter terms, when the "big boys" attended. During the fall and spring terms only younger children attended; their older sisters and brothers were employed on the farms; and even during the winter term some "big boys" were permitted to come late.

I had heard about fights between teachers and "big boys"; but in my day I witnessed only one whipping, when "teacher" easily handled the "tough." I do not recall a single case in which a school director was called on to interfere, nor do I recall having heard a pupil "sass" the teacher. During the noon recess, a club was thrown against the schoolhouse, damaging the weatherboarding. After having tried in vain to find out who was the offender, on the following day the teacher kept the "big boys" in their seats while the rest of us ate our lunches. After a stern lecture that failed to bring forth a confession, every boy in turn was required to rise and say: "I did not throw that stick against the schoolhouse." Every boy did. I was later informed that the guilty boy boasted that he said: "I did ought throw that stick against the schoolhouse."

The curriculum was simple and remained the same year after year. Copies of textbooks were used by several members of the family, and by the time they were handed down to me they were frayed, torn, and scribbled. The subjects taught were reading, spelling, arithmetic, geography, United States history, physiology, and penmanship. Two or three advanced pupils studied grammar—if they requested it. Once or twice a week a brief period was set aside for the singing of Gospel Hymns, but there was no formal instruction in music. Pupils had the privilege of suggesting hymns. In the estimation of the school population the best pupils excelled in arithmetic and spelling. It was a real achievement to "work all the examples" and to spell down the school. In geography we learned the states and territories of the United States and their capitals and principal cities. I could "bound" every state and territory and locate the principal rivers and lakes. We learned something about the population, resources, and topography of the states and foreign countries and about the customs and occupations of the peoples of the world.

The pattern of instruction and routine did not vary from term to term, except in the instance of a teacher who was fresh out of a business college, where he had become an expert in rapid calculation—mental arithmetic—and an enthusiast for "muscular movement" penmanship. Not content with having us fill the pages of our copybooks with ovals and flourishes of the pen, he also sent home with every pupil a double-page sheet of foolscap paper with instructions to fill every line with one or more words which he had written at the top of the page. He made no distinction between the ages of his pupils. At the age of eight I was required to cover the same amount of paper that was required of boys and girls twice my age and the papers had to be written between Friday afternoon and Monday morning. My papers were stained with tears and blots. On one occasion the teacher exhibited before the entire school a paper of mine that was disfigured with two huge blots — and was my face red. The pedagogue even called that to the attention of the school. Perhaps it was the memory of that humiliation that caused me to express a preference for women teachers.

I have a vivid recollection of another incident of my early school days. After school "was out" boys and girls walked to their respective homes in groups; and one afternoon the "big boys" incited me to throw clods at the girls. My aim was so accurate that when I approached our front gate, my Mother met me with a switch that was applied as soon as we entered the house. She had been informed of my misconduct by my sister who did not loiter, as I did. The humiliation of being led into the house in plain sight of my schoolmates was greater than the whipping. Upon reflection, I believe the whip ought to have been used on the boys who "put me up to it"; but at the time I did not feel that the punishment was unjust. I had complete confidence in my Mother's judgment; and it was probably wholesome to be made to understand early in life that the individual must take responsibility for his own actions. The only educational philosophy I ever heard my Father expound was summed up in the following sentence: "If you ever get a whipping in school, you'll get a harder one at home."

The "last day of school" —the end of the term— called for special exercises. We dressed in our Sunday clothes in honor of visitors, who were not numerous. The regular routine was followed in the forenoon; and in the afternoon each pupil "spoke a piece," which was usually selected by a member of the family. In the absence of report cards that recorded our grades, we were presented with souvenir cards autographed by the teacher.

Without disparaging the instruction gained in school and its wholesome influence, my fundamental education was a product of the home. My parents had been deprived of the opportunity of attending school and had an almost sacred respect for the public school. They never interfered with or questioned the judgment of the teacher. It was enough to know that their children were regular in attendance, kept out of trouble, and made progress. For many years Oliver was a school director and treasurer, but in my day he never visited school.

The library in our home was modest. Most of the books were devotional. The family Bible was conspicuous on the marble top table in the sitting room—and it was read. Another book in daily use was a volume of daily devotions written by the great pietist and lay preacher, Carl Olof Rosenius of Sweden. 'The "Rosenius book" was read in the family circle almost every evening, with members of the family taking turns, not excepting the youngest member. On Sunday forenoons when roads were impassable on account of snow or mud, the family assembled to hear the reading of what seemed to me a long sermon for the appropriate Sunday in a volume of Swedish homilies. Sometimes Oliver would request a member of the family to finish the reading. At the conclusion of the service, we were free to turn to our own devices, with the understanding that there would be no disturbance of the peace of the Sabbath by unnecessary noises. I thought Sundays were dreary unless we had company, and that was more often than not.

Next to the Bible, Mary's favorite books were Bunyan's *Pilgrim's Progress* and Von Schmidt's *Genoveva*, both in Swedish translation. She also read the weekly organ published by the church and Swedish secular weekly papers. Oliver was a regular reader of the Bible; and even before we left the farm, which was before my tenth birthday, he paid me a dollar for reading the New Testament in Swedish. After we moved to the city when he was relieved of the duties of the farm, almost every afternoon I sat at his side while we read alternate verses of three or four chapters of the Swedish Bible. Such "cruel and unusual punishment" is supposed to turn the victim forever away from Holy Scripture; but it had the ultimate effect of stimulating my interest in several versions of the Bible.

Except for the *Chicago Daily Drovers Journal* that Oliver subscribed to about that time of the year when his cattle and hogs were ready for market, our information about national and world events was obtained from the inside pages of a weekly Mount Pleasant paper and from

Swedish weeklies published in Chicago. It wasn't until shortly before we left the farm, in January 1894, that the post office at Swedesburg received daily mail, which was brought in a hack from Mount Pleasant. Before that, there were three mail deliveries a week. Neighbors called for mail that was delivered on the return trip. Farmers in Henry County did not enjoy the advantage of rural free delivery until the last year or two of the nineteenth century and by that time some of them had the convenience of telephones. Oliver lived until 1898, but he never spoke into a telephone transmitter. I doubt that he ever heard a phonograph.

We were indebted to our closest neighbors for the luxury of reading back numbers of the *Century Magazine* and *Harper's Monthly Magazine*. This family had moved from Ohio— "back East," they called it—and must have seen better days, otherwise they could not have afforded to subscribe to these expensive periodicals. I was not allowed to handle the copies without supervision, to make sure they would be returned in good condition. These good neighbors constantly borrowed money from Oliver; and it may be that the loan of the magazines was intended to be compound interest.

Their hired hand, who was also from Ohio, was my first "source material" for the Civil War. He was with Sherman on his march through Georgia. More than once I was put to bed when he was in the midst of a battle in which the "plague-gonned rebels" were routed by the charge on their "earthworks." His other favorite topic of conversation was a span of mules that took the bit in their teeth and tore down the road "like a bat out of hell," as he expressed it.

Among the volumes in our bookcase were novels by Dickens, Scott, Hawthorne, Willkie Collins and E. P. Roe, Eugene Sue's *The Wandering Jew*, Defoe's *Robinson Crusoe*, and of course, Mrs. Stowe's *Uncle Tom's Cabin*. My sister and I prized finely illustrated paper-bound copies of *Little Red Riding Hood*, *Jack the Giant Killer*, and

Bluebeard, which we obtained from a wholesale concern in Chicago by cutting out a number of trade marks on packages of coffee.

A little book that made a strong impression on me was entitled Little Meg's Children, which was printed and distributed by the American Tract Society. It was the story of a little girl who was entrusted by her dying mother to care for two younger children until their sailor father returned from a long voyage. The names of places in London were strange to an Iowa boy; and it was even stranger to a boy who had never seen a drunken man, much less a drunken woman (whose disreputable life I did not understand), to read about the poverty and wretchedness of the slums in England's metropolis. Accustomed as I was to the comforts and bounties of an Iowa farm, it did not occur to me that abject poverty could exist in the United States. To this day I remember little Meg's fortitude and faith in God; strangers who befriended her; and the rescue of Kitty from her sinful life by her mother, who found her through errands of mercy to the wretched tenement of little Meg and her children. Similar "good deed" stories in McGuffey's readers have remained lifelong memories. I have also a vivid memory of the sluggard in the Third Reader—in ragged clothing, leaning against the awry gate, with the dilapidated house in the background.

My first venture into the profession of writing was inspired by the patent medicine almanacs that hung under the clock shelf in the kitchen. The almanacs were published by four firms, respectively; but those consulted most frequently by Oliver were put out by Jayne and Ayer and were also printed in Swedish translation. I found them interesting: the dates of eclipses of the sun and moon; the moon's phases; the signs of the Zodiac; the lists of historic events and the dates of the births of famous people; the weather forecasts; the humorous items at the foot of the page; and the testimonials about the curative properties of sarsaparilla, hair tonic, cough syrup, and pills.

My ambition to edit an almanac would probably not have borne fruit but for the fortunate circumstance that my oldest brother had recently purchased a general merchandise store in Swedesburg. His stock included patent medicines. He presented me with a pad of letter-size wrapping paper, on one side of which was printed an advertisement of a patent medicine. That solved the problem of obtaining paper—writing paper in our home was too valuable to be wasted—and for some time I was occupied with making almanacs, Swedish and English, weather predictions and all. One of my sisters bound them by sewing the sheets together and attaching loops by which my almanacs could hang under the clock shelf with the others. Every morning, for a time at least, I consulted my own weather forecasts, which did not come off too badly in comparison with the "authorized" publications.

I was also indebted to my merchant brother for discarded journals and ledgers that were kept by his predecessor. These books contained blank, or partially blank, pages that were used for my first venture into the dubious business of keeping a diary. Of the inception of this ambition I am not clear, unless it was the example set by Oliver who occasionally recorded events, personal and otherwise, in memorandum books distributed by manufacturers of farm implements.

Before we left the farm, my youngest sister and I launched an undertaking in journalism. It was a weekly entitled "The Budget of News" —suggested by my partner. The editors assumed responsibility for publication in alternate weeks. The columns of the sheet were filled with local news pertaining to imaginary communities and "jokes." In my editorials, I fear the "jokes" were plagiarized from the almanacs, and the weekly papers. The publication of the "Budget" was continued after we moved to the city, where news was more abundant.

I have stated that there was no formal instruction in music in the district school; but Oliver and Mary loved music and provided our home with a fine reed organ. Mary played only simple hymns—winsome songs dear to the pietistic in Sweden. Many nights my eyes closed in sleep while my sisters and brothers, and sometimes visiting young folks, sang such familiar Gospel Hymns as "Whiter than the Snow," "Bringing in the Sheaves," "Rescue the Perishing," and "Jesus, Lover of my Soul." My sisters took music lessons from an itinerant German teacher.

A topic of conversation in homes and on the school grounds was the addition of a piano to our home. There may have been rural homes outside the Swedish community blessed with this instrument, but ours was the first Swedish home to have that distinction. On the afternoon of the day the piano was delivered, the homecoming school children loitered at our front gate to hear the tones of the strange instrument; and I dashed into the parlor to see what a piano looked like. A piano in the parlor and a reed organ in the sitting room was really something, I thought, and perhaps the neighbors thought so, too.

I have said nothing about the church as an educational institution; but in our family it claimed as much attention as the school. Mary's supervision guaranteed that her children came to Sunday school prepared to recite the lessons in Bible history and to repeat verbatim the assignments in Luther's Catechism. Self-respect, if nothing more, dictated that her children would be spared the humiliation of coming to class unprepared.

V
SOCIAL LIFE IN SWEDESBURG: CHURCH, SCHOOL AND HOME

Even in the early years of the Swedish settlement, 'green Swedes' won the hands of daughters of prosperous American farmers.

I have stated that the community in which I was born was the United States of America in miniature. The Swedish settlement took its inception in 1865 with the arrival of immigrants--among them my parents-- who purchased land in Wayne Township. In the following year the Swedish Lutheran Congregation was organized at Swedesburg. Several of the charter members came from New Sweden in Jefferson County, and others moved in from Illinois. They chose one of their number to act as agent to give advice and assistance to countrymen who might be attracted to the settlement. Through the columns of a Swedish weekly which circulated among the churchly Swedes, the agent gave the location of the community, the quality and price of land, and facilities for timber and water.

A cordial invitation was extended to immigrants who took religious advantages into account and wished to be edified by the Word of God. Those who were hostile and antagonistic toward the religious life and the Lutheran doctrine were advised to go elsewhere. A Sunday school had been organized; a site for a church had already been selected; and a minister from New Sweden, some fourteen miles away, conducted services every third Sunday. "The other Sundays," the agent wrote, "we gather around the Word which is truth and can

Swedish Lutheran Church
1883-1926
Destroyed by Fire

make us wise unto salvation." At the time the communication was written, in 1866, there were about twenty Swedes who owned land and a few who rented land. From these small beginnings grew one of the largest and most prosperous Swedish communities in the United States.

The social life of the community was built around the church, the school, and the home. Our farm was on the western edge of the settlement, which encroached on the German Amish community. To the east of the Swedish settlement was a Quaker settlement; but I knew nothing about it, except that I heard my brothers talk about the Quaker meeting they had attended and that the "Quaker preacher," as he was called, was a good friend of my Father and was not infrequently in our home. He was a queer preacher, I thought, because he wore no distinctive garb, as did the Lutheran clergyman—not even a Prince Albert coat—and he would even take a drink of whiskey which Oliver poured from a bottle which he kept in the pantry for occasions when good friends dropped in, or when on a cold day a farmer stopped in to get warm on his return from "the timber" with a load of wood.

The bottle and the small silver cups were never brought out except on very special occasions; and never was liquor served at dinners, when a long table was set for guests. I thought it unusual for Oliver to address the Quaker preacher by his given name. That would have been unthinkable in the case of the Lutheran minister. The Amish preacher and Oliver were also close friends and addressed each other by their given names. Perhaps the explanation lies in the fact that the Quaker and the Amish preachers were farmers.

We had many contacts with the Amish. They were prompt in paying their debts and invariably returned a plow or a mower or a harrow on the day promised—so Oliver said. Their houses and barns were well painted, and their yards were flower gardens. If lightning struck and burned down a barn, or if a horse died, neighbors contributed labor and money to make up for the loss. Except for certain expressions that were strange to us, we did not look upon them as "foreigner". It did sound strange to hear them speak of "forty-second cousins"; but their plain costumes evoked no comment, although in later years, after we had left the farm, I heard them referred to as "hook-and-eye Dutch."

Visiting with the Amish seemed to be an all-day affair; at least some families came in the forenoon and stayed all day. In later years I heard my sisters tell how the Amish girls of their own age "tried on" their hats before a mirror—always making sure that their elders were at a safe distance. The Amish maids had small cause to envy my sisters. It is true that they wore hats adorned with flowers and feathers; but they dressed in accord with Mary's wishes and with the Apostle Paul's admonition that women adorn themselves in modest apparel. Piety, economy, and provincialism were levelers. It is true that city folks who on rare occasions visited their country cousins were envied for their finery. Little did the rustic maidens and young men realize that the objects of their envy could little afford their dresses with long trains and their haberdashery.

Surrounding the Swedish settlement on the north, east, and south were descendants of native American stock. The Swedes called them "Yankees" and "Americans." To the Americans, the Swedes must have appeared "foreign" or "outlandish," but there was never serious friction or fighting between "gangs." I heard Oliver speak of certain "Swede-haters," but they were exceptional. On one occasion a Swede hater played the role of a "road hog" and held up a long procession of Swedes who were returning from Mount Pleasant after having delivered hogs to market. The "road hog" was put in his proper place when the Swedes pulled up at the side of the road and made way for

Oliver to pass them and catch up with the offender. This incident was related to me some years after Oliver's death.

There was of course a certain clannishness among the Swedes, which might have been the product of a superiority complex or of an inferiority complex—if there is such a distinction. There was a disposition to look up to their American neighbors: to envy their natural American manners and their familiarity with the customs of the country and to seek their advice. Some of them had served their apprenticeships as American farmers in the employ of Americans who paid them well, treated them with consideration, taught them the rudiments of English, and perhaps helped them to become freeholders. Even in the early years of the Swedish settlement, "green Swedes" won the hands of daughters of prosperous American farmers.

On the school grounds Americans, Germans, and Swedes mingled on equal terms. I do not recall hearing the epithets "Dutch" and "Swede" bandied, not even in the case of a Swedish immigrant eighteen or twenty years of age who started with the *First Reader* and sat with the children on the bench at the front of the room to recite the lesson. It did seem strange for me to be using the *Third Reader*; but I remembered having heard our "newcomer" hired hands, who were even older than me, spell words in the *First Reader* and read the childish stories about Mary and Lucy. We laughed over these incidents, and so did the "newcomers."

There were of course rivalries, jealousies, and feuds between families that revealed themselves in school; but they were not rooted in race or nationality. "Sectionalism" was manifest in a certain hostility between children who lived east of the schoolhouse and those who resided to the west; but it never reached the stage of open warfare. Girls as well as boys played baseball; and in "choosing up sides" there was no evidence of "sectionalism." The school brought families in closer contact. By previous arrangement, children stayed overnight in our home, and it was customary to return the compliment.

The schoolhouse was used for meetings of the "literary society" on Friday or Saturday nights. These meetings attracted young people from other school districts. I was not old enough to attend, but I heard my brothers and sisters speak of " going to literary"; and when schoolmates stayed overnight with us, we sometimes "played literary". These societies elected the usual officers; and their programs consisted of declamations, debates, extemporaneous speeches, readings, singing, and dialogues. Only once did I attend a "spelling down" contest, which was held in the evening. Young and old sat on benches that lined the wall of the schoolhouse. When the contest began, the contestants arose and remained standing until they were spelled down.

Only occasionally was the schoolhouse made available to itinerant entertainers. My initiation into this form of amusement was a performance by a ventriloquist, whose repertoire also included a Punch and Judy show. It frightened me to hear the man confined in the violin case converse with the ventriloquist and beg to be let out. For some time I had the poor man in my thoughts and in my dreams.

The bicycle craze, which was at its height in the decade of the nineties, invaded our community before we left the farm, in January 1894. One of my brothers created a mild sensation in the summer of the previous year by bringing his bicycle with him on a visit to his parental home. Bicycles were luxuries on the farm; but even if that consideration had not been serious, the condition of the roads -- dust, ruts, mud, and steep grades -- made travel by that means anything but a pleasure, as I learned a few years later when I rode my bicycle sixteen miles from a railroad station to the home of my uncle, who resided on a farm not far from our old homestead. Even horses that I met on the road shied at the two-wheeled vehicle.

The Church and the Rosenians

The Swedish Lutheran Church was the social center of the community. It was a large frame edifice, painted white, with a steeple that on a clear day could be seen at a great distance; and on a still Saturday evening when the bell tolled for the Sabbath, it could be heard on our farm, which was at a distance of about three miles. The uncommonly tall spire gave the church a distinction above that of any church in the county. The cemetery was in the churchyard; and the parsonage was just across the road.

Among the members of the Swedesburg Lutheran Church, the children of the Rosenian revival placed a stamp on the settlement. Rosenius was a great religious leader who remained a layman all his life, rather than to entangle himself in the meshes of the Church of Sweden. He saw the good, as well as the serious faults, in the established church and believed that through the activity of laymen the life of the Spirit could be breathed into it. His loyalty to Lutheran doctrine was steadfast; but he departed from the typical parish pastor by emphasizing the practical side of religion, a characteristic of American Protestantism. In fact, Rosenius was strongly influenced by the remarkable revival that swept over the United States in 1857 and 1858. In this revival, which was mainly the work of laymen, prayer was more important than preaching; and the activity of men and women was manifested by personal visitation and the distribution of tracts.

Sweden was flooded with American devotional literature, which in translation had a powerful influence on the humble folk from whom the great mass of the emigrants were recruited. Rosenius was also the beneficiary of substantial financial support from Christian associations in the United States, without which he could not have carried on his publication activity. The Rosenian movement, therefore, bore an American stamp. Unlike the parish clergy, who despised the American religious influence, Rosenius and his followers saw in the United States the most Christian country in the world and acknowledged their indebtedness to their brethren in America for inspiration, example, and material support.

The Rosenians were not vociferous in their religious exercises. Their informal meetings for Scripture reading and prayer were in tune with the winsome and appealing songs that brought comfort to pioneer homes. Prayer meetings in which young and old participated were held in homes in the Swedesburg community. In Sweden such gatherings were frowned upon by the clergy, partly because they were manifestations of democracy in church and state; but in the United States there were no conventicle acts which could be invoked against pietists and frequenters of conventicles.

The Rosenians were puritanical, and in the Swedesburg community some of them went to extremes in opposing a band which was organized in the eighties and by frowning on singing societies in which young people, regardless of church affiliation, met in homes to sing religious and secular songs. Certain musical instruments were associated with dancing and "worldly" social gatherings in the old country; and singing societies might wean the young from the church of their fathers or dilute their Lutheran orthodoxy.

There were of course individuals who strayed from the straight and narrow path or dropped their membership in the church; but scoffers, drunkards, and lawbreakers did not thrive in the puritanical atmosphere. The Rosenians had already imbibed the spirit of America before they took out permits to emigrate. There is a close parallel between the English Puritans of the seventeenth century and the Swedish pietists of the nineteenth. The Rosenians had as long a list of forbidden things of the world as did the New England Puritans. Both groups recoiled against an established church which had become a body of frigid mechanical forms and ceremonies, quenched the spirit, and gave the people only the dry husks of formalism.

Visitors from Sweden were often misled by outward appearances into thinking that the social life in communities like Swedesburg was drab and uninteresting; but my own experiences and observations testify to the contrary. There was virtue in hard work. Self-respect inspired wholesome rivalry to raise fine crops, to build comfortable homes, to improve farms, and to win the confidence of neighbors. America represented an ideal, and the ideal was not disillusioning. Memories of childhood and youth in Sweden lingered; but in America the future beckoned to a status of independence. Work was honorable; humiliating class distinctions did not exist; and children enjoyed opportunities that been denied to their parents.

It is true that many Swedish-American farmers were hard-headed and tight-fisted; but contributions to church and charity were not slighted in favor of luxuries and trivialities. Their outlook on life, well-being, and happiness must be interpreted in terms of their background of poverty, toil, and ambition.

In the absence of twentieth-century entertainments and amusements, horse and church were close to the hearts of young and old. The home was an institution. Large families were the rule, and every member was obligated to make sacrifices in terms of time, work, clothing, play, and money. Social life was inseparable from the family. The isolation of the farmstead assured a welcome to visitors, and even to strangers. In time of trouble, sickness, and death, families were dependent on neighbors. Mothers and daughters spent weeks—even months—in the homes of neighbors taking care of the sick; and children were treated as members of neighboring families when mothers were laid low by sickness and when parents were taken by death. The aged and the feeble had the privilege of staying for weeks in homes, moving from home to home at their pleasure. Social service was an individual responsibility, especially in the case of those in the same household of faith.

Christmas in Swedesburg

Christmas was the most festive and joyous season of the year. As in Sweden, in the Swedesburg community Christmas lasted for twenty days. Christmas Eve was the happiest day for the children. For days, and even weeks, preceding Christmas the women were busy cleaning every nook and corner of the house, making pots and kettles spick and span, preparing very special viands and delicacies, baking cookies decorated with red sugar, making shopping expeditions, and finally bathing the children with ruthless thoroughness. Then, if ever, the home and every member must be spotlessly clean. Cattle, horses, sheep, hogs, and chickens were given extra rations on Christmas Eve. Stalls were bedded with an unusual thickness of hay or straw.

In the days preceding Christmas I was many times reminded that Santa Claus knew every move I made and that it behooved me to conduct myself in accordance with his wishes. Until I was past my sixth birthday I had never been in a store to see a display of Christmas merchandise; and nobody could have convinced me that anybody but Santa Claus manufactured Christmas presents.

My acquaintance with him was limited to pictures and to information furnished by my parents and sisters and brothers. In my childhood, Santa did not stand at street corners ringing a bell, nor did he grant interviews to children who were bewildered by lavish displays in department stores. I knew from experience that Santa Claus was generous; but I was warned that he did not look with favor on selfish and greedy children. That warning was impressed on me by several stories, one of which was about an older brother who hung up two stockings, one of which was filled but the other was never found.

On Christmas Eve, after the livestock had been fed and shut up for the night, the men dressed for the occasion; and after what seemed to me an interminable wait, the family sat down to an early supper, which gave us the first taste of lutfisk for the season. After the dishes were washed and the table was set for breakfast, the doorbell rang furiously, whereupon ensued a rush for the door. Invariably a well-filled gunny bag was found on the porch. Santa Claus departed as mysteriously as he came.

Compared with the children of later generations, my assortment of presents was modest, but I was never disappointed. I had the assurance that Santa Claus put forth his best effort. In addition to toys, games, and wearing apparel, he brought candy, oranges, and nuts. It was only during the Christmas season that we enjoyed such luxuries as oranges, Brazil nuts, English walnuts, and pecans; and only rarely were bananas seen in our home.

After the presents had been distributed, the family retired early in order to be up betimes for Christmas matins which began at four o'clock. After a cup of coffee and rusks, the family was on the way to church. If the ground was covered with snow, the trip was made in bobsleds; if not, the three-seated platform buggy and a top buggy supplied transportation. Candles burned in the windows of Swedish homes as we drove by, and the plain windows of the church were illuminated by candles. At the conclusion of matins, a ten-minute recess intervened until the reed organ sounded the first hymn of the regular Sunday morning service, which lasted until seven o'clock.

In Sweden and in some Swedish-American communities it was customary for certain families to whip up the horses in order to beat the neighbors home; but in the Swedesburg community the day was too sacred for levity. In some "worldly" Swedish communities, the Christmas season was a time for drinking, carousing, end dancing; but if there were such homes in my boyhood community, they were not in conformity with the spirit of the Rosenians.

A substantial breakfast was prepared after returning from church, and a sumptuous dinner followed in the afternoon. There was a service at 10:30-o'clock on Christmas Day, but time and distance made it impossible for our family to attend. The observance of the day followed the pattern of Sunday, and generally our home was crowded with visitors, invited and uninvited.

The three weeks of the Christmas season brought many parties and feasts. The dinners were elaborate affairs and placed heavy burdens on the womenfolk. These affairs were somewhat cliquish, in that every year certain families were invited; and it was expected that the compliment would be returned. The "old folks" ate at the "first table"; but the fare at the "second table" was as elaborate as at the first. In the afternoon the parents and some of the young ladies sat through the reading of a long sermon by a deacon. If the minister was present, he led the group in Scripture reading and prayer and perhaps delivered a brief sermon. The children were allowed to amuse themselves; and the young men, for a time, repaired to the barn to smoke or chew tobacco. Oliver provided a box of cigars for these occasions, and most of the men were equipped with pipes.

The Sunday school program, which began at six o'clock, was reserved for Twelfth Night. Every boy and girl "spoke a piece" or sang a song. Groups of children stood in line at the front of the church; and after each individual effort, the superintendent presented a card and moved along to the next performer.

It was customary to engage one or two theological students to assist the pastor during the holidays; and they would have felt slighted if they had not been asked to address the children. With a notable exception or two, every part of the program was conducted in the Swedish language.

At the conclusion of the exercises, candy end apples

were distributed. There was always a Christmas tree in church; but Santa Claus was never permitted to set foot inside the church. In fact, he was never even mentioned. It would have been sacrilegious to allow him to intrude on a sacred program.

Swedish School

Sunday school was conducted only during the warm months of the year. My first and only teacher was a simple farmer who was unable to spell my name when I enrolled; and ever since I have been curious to know what he wrote even after I had spelled it for him. He liked boys, and we liked him. After the lesson in the Catechism had been recited, he told us stories and warned us of the wrath to come if we were disobedient. He made no effort to portray the horrors of hell; but I knew that good boys were rewarded in this world and in the next.

It was the fate of children of bilingual parents to attend Swedish summer school, which was held in the church and was conducted by a theological student or by a college student. The curriculum included the Catechism, Bible history, and reading. The purpose of the instruction was to teach the fundamentals of the Christian religion and to continue Swedish as a spoken language. Swedish school was not a "parochial school" in the sense that it was intended to compete with or supplant the public school. Parents found no fault with the public schools. They were prized among the great advantages which America provided their children. Moreover, the fact that from the beginning the Swedish Lutherans adopted the American Sunday school proves that they were Americans in spirit, if not in speech, before they left the Old Country. At the time of the founding of the Swedesburg settlement, and for some years thereafter, Sunday schools were sparsely distributed in Sweden.

Language and Literacy

Almost without exception, the Swedesburg settlers were recruited from the rural population of Sweden and had not attained the distinction of having surnames. Nels Andersson was the son of Anders Petersson, whose father's given name was Peter. So it went from father to son. In the United States this custom was discontinued. Nels Andersson's children retained the name "Anderson" by dropping one "s". Not only did the immigrants rise to the dignity of having surnames, but the adopted country also conferred on them the first titles they had ever had. They were addressed as "Mister," which placed them on an equality with bankers and merchants.

The women probably appreciated the American equality in speech and dress even more than did the men. Their work was more in keeping with feminine taste; and they, too, were addressed as "Mrs." or "Miss."

No language teacher can ever instruct the third generation in the spoken language of the first generation of Swedes in the United States. Few immigrants spoke pure Swedish. Their speech was a provincial dialect, and within a remarkably short time it metamorphosed into a ludicrous combination of Swedish dialect and English, which could be understood neither by an American nor by a recent arrival from Sweden. Swedish words in common use were the first to go in favor of such words as stove, farm, machine, buggy, knife, barn, chickens, and the like. "No" and "yes" were immediately added to the vocabulary. "Going to church" became "going to meeting."

In order to advertise their proficiency in the language of the adopted country to friends and relatives in Sweden, immigrants injected English words, usually incorrectly spelled, in their letters. Not only were liberties taken with English nouns but innocent Swedish words were mutilated beyond recognition. The spelling of place names in the United States defied efforts to locate them on the map, even if the persons to whom the letters were addressed had possessed an atlas, which was unlikely. After the passing of another generation, or possibly two generations, the letters will be unreadable.

In the early years of the immigration movement the letters were written by men and women who grew to maturity before Sweden provided the advantages of popular education. Their spoken language was the dialect of the province that gave them birth; and their knowledge of reading and writing was the product of instruction in the home, supplemented by the instruction for catechumens by the parish pastor. The person who has the patience to spell his way through the "America letters," however, cannot fail to have a profound respect for the ability of the writers to express themselves and for their sound and wholesome instincts. They reveal that both in their native and adopted countries they thought seriously about their own problems and about those of their adopted countries.

VI
THE MOVE TO THE CITY

I was told that electric street cars ran on the street on which our house was situated, but that conjured up no images in the mind of a boy who had never seen an electric light or a vehicle other than a wagon, buggy, or carriage.

In the fall of 1893, Oliver made the surprising decision to leave the farm in favor of the city. The reason he gave for this extraordinary decision was that he wanted to provide better educational advantages for his children. There were, however, other reasons. In the summer of 1891, his beloved Mary passed away after a lingering illness. The farm which had been his home since 1865 could never be the same without the patient, self-sacrificing, God-fearing partner who had shared the hardships of a primitive home and had later enjoyed the comforts of prosperity.

The duties of the farm were discharged with the same hard-driving energy; but Oliver was in his sixtieth year, and his two older sons had left the farm in order to venture into the general merchandise business in northwestern Iowa.

Changes in Swedesburg

During the first nine years of my life, I had the good fortune to enjoy the peace, security, and prosperity of Henry County, Iowa. I have since seen the number of tombstones in the Swedesburg cemetery increase from year to year. I have, seen another generation grow up. The "big white church" was struck by a bolt of lightning and burned to the ground. A brick edifice, with a basement, Sunday school rooms, pipe organ, and electric lights, now attracts the attention of motorists who speed over the paved highway. The hitching posts that surrounded the churchyard have been removed, as has also the stile, which enabled the womenfolk to alight gracefully and safely from platform buggies and spring wagons.

"The Swedish Evangelical Lutheran Church" has been renamed "Swedesburg Evangelical Lutheran Church" to indicate that it is a "community" church whose membership is not restricted to persons who understand Swedish. The Sunday school and confirmation classes are conducted exclusively in the language of the country. Only an occasional Swedish service is held out of respect for the few members who crave the hymns of the Swedish Prayerbook and sermons in the language of the ministers who formerly occupied the pulpit. In the album published in commemoration of the seventy-fifth anniversary, the roster of members includes such surnames as Canby, Coughlin, Goodrich, Kennedy, Morrow, Riepe, Rinner, and Roth; and among the given names appear Leslie, Rupert, LeRoy, Lloyd, Chester, Maynard, Prudence, Darlene, Marcile, Marjorie, Jean, and June.

The triumph of English over Swedish was a natural and gradual transition. The older generation held to Swedish, and the younger generation was a bit impatient; but there were no organized groups to generate discord, nor was there organized propaganda from outside the congregation. Down to the closing years of the last century it was assumed by leaders in the church that Swedish would continue to be the language of worship so far into the future that it was unnecessary to prepare for the transition to English. This attitude was perhaps typical of foreign-language churches. The miracles of the twentieth century were in a sealed book even to men and women whose span of life extended into its early years.

In my boyhood the county seat was so remote that some members of the family visited it no more often than twice a year. A few young men who had endured the inconveniences of a ride in a caboose on a "stock pass" had unbelievable stories to tell about the skyscrapers in

Chicago; and in the year before I left the farm fabulously low railroad rates attracted an unusually large number of farm hands to the World's Columbian Exposition in the western metropolis. Even this sensational attraction did not' tempt Oliver to visit the city to which he came as an immigrant in 1849, when a steamboat brought him to what became the greatest railroad center in the world. He lived within about two hundred miles of the city throughout his lifetime, but never saw its greatness.

My first "jogerfy book" which became outmoded before I left the district school listed among the territories North Dakota, South Dakota, Washington, Montana, Idaho, and Wyoming. Indian Territory suggested that there was still a frontier, but it is doubtful if that word was ever used by teacher or pupil in geography and history classes.

In spite of' depressions that followed the panics of 1873 and 1893, the Swedish farmers in Henry County moved toward the goal of economic security, which was attained by industry, economy, self-denial, and rising land values. When Oliver left the community, well-improved farms with good buildings and drainage sold for as much as fifty or sixty dollars per acre; but his neighbors thought him too optimistic when he predicted that some day land would sell for one hundred dollars an acre. The prophecy was fulfilled in 1905, when his own farm sold for exactly that amount. During the boom years preceding and immediately following the First World War, land values soared to fantastic heights.

But I am not much interested in the material development of the Swedesburg community. I think of it as a home from which I have never been absent. A new generation has come to which I am a stranger, but the memories of boyhood have priority.

Becoming "The New Kid"

I was too young to have a part in the activities that

preceded the family migration to the city. The two auction sales that attracted farmers from near and far linger in my memory. I accompanied Oliver to the job-printing establishment in Mount Pleasant where he left the manuscript for the poster announcing the first sale. When we called for the finished product, I noticed that the name of the auctioneer was incorrectly spelled, which delayed us until the revised version was ruin through the press. My first experience in reading proof was commended by Oliver.

In the fall and early winter Oliver made trips to Rock Island, Illinois, where our future residence was under construction. I saw the plan of the house and heard members of the family talk about new-fangled conveniences, such as a hot air furnace, running water in the kitchen, and a bathroom. I was told that electric street cars ran on the street on which our house was situated, but that conjured up no images in the mind of a boy who had never seen an electric light or a vehicle other than a wagon, buggy, or carriage.

On a bright winter day early in January 1894, our nearest neighbor furnished transportation and brought us to the railroad station, a distance of' sixteen miles. The passenger train had changed time, so there was no course other than to board a local freight train that left about noon and arrived in Rock Island after dark. In the morning I was awakened by the noise of vehicles and streetcars and realized that I had left behind the peace and quiet of Swedesburg. For some days I spent most of the time at the window watching pedestrians and delivery wagons. When I went out of doors, boys ventured into our yard to have a look at the "new kid," inquired where I came from, and asked what grade I was in. It wasn't until I enrolled in school that I understood what a grade was. I had no credentials from the district school, so I was assigned to the grade appropriate to my age.

VII
THE ACADEMY YEARS

The most difficult adjustment in the city was in the school.

In my new environment I was still a citizen of Swedish America. Rock Island was the capital of the Swedish Lutheran Church in America. It was the seat of the oldest Swedish-American educational institution, Augustana College and Theological Seminary, and of the church's publication house. My Father had served on the board of directors of the college and seminary; and as a member of the Swedesburg Sunday school I had "solicited" funds for the new building. The twin city of Moline, whose western boundary was only two blocks from our new home, had a much larger Swedish population than Rock Island. Swedish immigrants were attracted to Moline by factories, which turned out agricultural implements.

A Boy's Life in Rock Island

That part of Rock Island which became my home in January 1894, was a boy's paradise. Many vacant lots and large tracts that had not been subdivided into lots and cut up by streets afforded an extensive cruising range and improvised baseball "diamonds." Much of the land was heavily wooded; and there were no "Keep Out" signs and no irate property owners to deprive us of the privilege of gathering walnuts and butternuts and of filling our caps and pockets with red haws, chokecherries, and ash berries. During the spring and summer months our cow was pastured on property adjacent to our home, where she shared forage and the shade of the virgin forest with cows that belonged to neighbors.

There were no artificial skating rinks—at least I knew of none— but there were times when the Mississippi furnished excellent skating above what we called the "government dam". The most fun of all was coasting on bobsleds dawn the steep bluffs that skirted the river. There were no paved streets in our immediate vicinity, and there were no automobiles and trucks to make coasting hazardous. Even on principal streets there were so few buggies, delivery wagons, and other vehicles that there was little risk in the sport. After school and at night the street on which we lived was alive with children and teen-age boys and girls. At the cry of "track" from the throats of a half-dozen or more youngsters about to descend, the caravan of sleds moving in the opposite direction pulled aside to clear the track. Rarely did misunderstandings arise, although there was rivalry between parties over the distance covered. I have no recollection of a serious accident, in spite of many "spills."

Swimming was an "illegitimate" sport because there was no public beach where the safety of swimmers was guarded by employees and by precautions that today are taken for granted. We had to sneak away to the "swimming hole" and dry our hair before returning to our homes. Our "swimming hole" was in an arm of the Mississippi, which was called the "Slough", and at a place where the current was slowed up by the "government dam". I have no recollection of having been asked by a member of the family if I ever went swimming, nor do I recall having seen a single narrow escape from drowning. Our bathing beach was for "boys only," and it was so remote from beaten paths that swimming suits were unnecessary. Our greatest problem was how to "shake" a younger brother who was in the gang and to make sure that no "tattletale" was in on the secret.

Life at School

The most difficult adjustment in the city was in the school. The contrast between the size of the schoolhouse in the city and the one-room district school filled me with

awe. However, in the spirit of the Good Samaritan a neighbor boy who was a grade ahead of me made the first day of school easier than I anticipated. I was enrolled in the fifth grade. The children in the fifth and sixth grades occupied the same room and were taught by the same teacher. It seemed to me that the pupils were
unusually noisy; but that was because there were many more of them than there were in the district school.

    The schoolhouse was new and well equipped; and the teachers, with one mild exception, were competent. Except for rare visits by the music teacher, the drawing teacher, and the calisthenics teacher, the instruction was exclusively in the hands of the teachers assigned to the respective rooms. There was no school nurse. I was informed that I had to have a vaccination certificate, so my Father brought me to a physician in Moline who apparently did not take the requirement seriously. He informed us that the virus he had on hand had probably lost its potency; but he scratched my arm, applied the virus, and handed me a certificate, for which he received a fee of fifty cents. The fee proved to be exorbitant, figured in terms of results

    I still have in my possession my report cards for the fifth, seventh, and eighth grades. In comparing these reports cards with the report cards of my two sons in the Minneapolis Public Schools, some thirty-five years later, I find that the subjects listed are similar, with the addition of social studies, manual training, and orchestra. They were marked on conduct and effort; I was graded on deportment. My sons brought home dental certificates, reports of eye tests, and reports of routine examinations, which were conducted by the hygiene department. In my day there was no suggestion of "socialized medicine and dentistry" in the Rock Island Public Schools.

    A slate was standard equipment for each pupil, and it was used chiefly for "number work." Except for examinations, there was little written work; and the word "project" was not in our vocabulary.

In the rural school there was only one teacher who began the day by reading a portion of the Bible and pupils and teachers joined in daily devotional exercises. The teacher read Scripture and all repeated the Lord's Prayer. I have just paged through a volume from the past entitled "The Public School Music Course Number Two" by G. R. Housel, published by the Rock Island Music Co., and found that religious songs greatly outnumber the secular. Another sign of changing times is the fact that from the music reader used in the ninth grade, by the same author, we sang "Die Wacht am Rhine" —in translation, of course.

The principal of the school, who also taught the ninth grade, was an excellent disciplinarian and teacher. One could sense that teachers and pupils alike respected her - and feared her. Our school had its share of "tough kids," but the principal knew how to deal with them without summoning help.

The teacher who was named as the "mild exception" had an inferiority complex and we knew it, but not by that name. She was probably the only college graduate on the teaching staff, a recent graduate of Augustana College, which was sometimes referred to disdainfully as the "Swede college." She was one of the few members of the Swedish population who had risen to the high distinction of initiation into the sorority of public school teachers in Rock Island. At the very beginning of the term her morale was shaken by her inept dealing with a surly boy who doubled up his fists and avowed that "no immigrant Swede" could talk like that to him. Throughout the entire school year I felt sorry for her. Somehow she didn't belong, and at the opening of the next school year her room was in charge of another teacher. About thirty years later I met her on the campus of Augustana College, only five blocks from the schoolhouse, and reminded her of the months she was my teacher. Without any reference to the episode just related she named the boy who was a thorn in her flesh.

Baseball

My first summer in Rock Island brought me into contact with professional baseball. The ballpark was only a block from my home; and I soon learned that there were means of admission other then by ticket. The most honorable way was by retrieving a foul ball that went over the fence; but the wait was tedious, and there was always the probability that the boy with the fleetest heels would have priority. By hook or crook, before the season was far advanced I had learned the lingo of the bleachers. The pitcher for the visiting team had a "glass arm"; the slow-moving base runner was an "ice wagon"; and after the umpire had called a base runner either "out" or "safe," somebody invariably shouted "twenty minutes for lunch!" If a man stood up and obstructed the view of the field, a "fan" would be sure to call out "Hey, is your old man a glassblower?"

Baseball as it was played in 1894 was different in some respects from the game as it was played a few years later. Until the beginning of the present century the catcher did not put on his mask until the batter had either two strikes or two or three balls, unless there was a man on base. Joe Cantillon, who managed the Rock Island team in 1894, later became an umpire in the National League when he suggested the rule compelling the catcher to "take off" behind the bat throughout the game. He is also credited with having suggested the foul strike rule, prior to which only a foul attempted sacrifice and a "tick foul" caught by the catcher were called strikes. The pitcher, who used no mitt, warmed up between innings by playing catch with the first baseman. After each pitch, the catcher gently returned the ball by rolling it to the pitcher, unless there was a man on base, when the pitcher walked toward the plate and caught an easy toss. There was only one umpire, which made it easy for a base runner to stretch a two-base hit into a triple by cutting second base by as much as ten feet.

In the years of depression following the panic of 1893, a number of minor leagues were disbanded or their circuits were changed by the dropping out of certain cities because of poor patronage. In 1895 the Rock Island ballpark was used for bicycle races; and at the end of the year the fence, bleachers, and grandstand were removed,

Discovering Politics

The following year the open space attracted a crowd of men and women far in excess of previous attractions. The magnet was William Jennings Bryan, the boy orator of the Platte, who in a frenzy of enthusiasm had been nominated for President of the United States by the Democratic convention in Chicago.

A platform was erected at the approximate center of the former ballpark. My companion and I arrived early and took a position as close to the platform as it was physically possible. Within a short time the platform was surrounded on all sides by people who had come to see and hear the youthful crusader for free silver. It would have been impossible for two boys to elbow their way to the outskirts of the multitude, so we made ourselves comfortable by crawling under the platform to relieve the fatigue of standing.

As a youngster not yet in his teens and brought up in a Swedish Lutheran home—for Swedish Lutheranism and Republicanism were identical twins—I could not join in the "Hurrahs!" for Bryan. From my Father, who had stored in his memory the accumulated sins of the Democratic party from James Buchanan to Grover Cleveland, I heard no words of praise for the man who been nominated by a Democratic convention and by its Populist ally, whose platforms gave sleepless nights to Republicans and old-line Democrats. Even the quartette which drew applause by singing "Rothschild's got the boodle, and

Uncle Sam's a noodle" did not appeal to me. A few days later I was badly disillusioned when I heard the same quartette sing Republican campaign songs at a Republican rally. Later in life I learned that men sang hosannas to party regularity for even more substantial rewards.

The presidential campaign of 1896 was especially interesting to me because both parties stressed the emotional appeal by elaborate torchlight parades, by lurid cartoons, and by the large assortment of campaign buttons worn by young and old.

I lived to see the day when the man who was berated as a "Popocrat," ridiculed as a lunatic, and condemned as an anarchist came into his own as a "Christian statesman." After his free silver heresy was almost forgotten and he was no longer a presidential possibility, fundamentalists at the time of the Scopes evolution trial in Tennessee claimed Bryan as their own; and crusaders for peace eulogized him for resigning as Secretary of State in Wilson's cabinet at the time of the Lusitania crisis.

The most extraordinary example in my lifetime of how contemporary opinions are nullified by time and intelligence is furnished by John P. Altgeld, the first Democratic governor of Illinois after the Civil War. In 1896 I saw cartoons which made Bryan's kindly and benevolent face appear to be a mask for "Altgeldism," anarchism, and repudiation. I have a faint recollection of the excitement caused by Coxey's army in 1894, the year we moved to Rock Island. More vivid in my memory is the Pullman strike, which in the early months of that year paralyzed railroad traffic through Chicago. As a boy of ten I did not understand the inception of the strike and the issues involved. I saw headlines blazing the names of Altgeld, Pullman, and Cleveland and at home and abroad I heard nothing but praise for Cleveland and condemnation for Altgeld. It seemed unreal to hear words of praise for a Democratic President from my Father. "Cleveland is a good man in bad company," he said.

Altgeld was buried under an avalanche of misrepresentation and irresponsible journalism. But about thirty years after he had been driven into political oblivion, two biographies presented the honest and courageous governor to a select list of readers. But the most astonishing reversal came fifty years later.

Newspaper editorials rejoiced that Catholic and Protestant bishops, more than a dozen present and past governors, senators, and congressmen, numerous heads of great corporations and publishers of great newspapers, and distinguished educators and jurists joined in honoring his memory. One editorial explained why Altgeld was "as revered today as he was reviled fifty years ago." It was because fair-minded men had come to see that Altgeld, the immigrant, was a true democrat and a great American, while his native-born assailants fell far short of the American concept of social justice and democratic liberty.

A paragraph in an editorial in the *Minneapolis Tribune* for December 29, 1947, might well be framed and displayed in every editorial department of newspapers, in every schoolhouse, and in the narthex of every church: "Had Altgeld been mindful of his own interests he would have maintained a Pontius Pilate attitude towards a social injustice not of his doing. Then Altgeld would have died well spoken of by his contemporaries and be forgotten today."

The Spanish American War

The year 1898 is associated with two major events in my life. It was in that year that I finished the first lap of my formal education by graduating from the grades; and it was in that year that the War with Spain began and ended. For weeks and months the headlines were bigger and bolder and wilder than they were in 1894. The boy who sat at the desk immediately in front of mine was a newsboy;

and every morning before school 'took up" he unfolded before my eyes a Chicago paper, whose headlines blazed forth sensational rumors and speculations worthy or unworthy, of the best or worst efforts of yellow journalism in the rival metropolis on the Atlantic Coast. One headline after the sinking of the "Maine" stands out almost as clearly as I write this as if the newspaper were before me: SPAIN WILL HAVE TO PAY $15, 000,000.

Vivid in my memory is an April day when we wondered what might be the meaning of the prolonged sounding of the many factory whistles in Moline at an unusual time of the day. There were no telephones in the homes of our neighbors, so I mounted my bicycle and within a few minutes joined the crowd before the bulletin board of the *Moline Dispatch* and read that Congress had declared war against Spain. On my way home I passed a home and heard hysterical weeping. Two Sons in that family were in the state militia.

About two weeks later the chorus of whistles was louder and more prolonged. The occasion was the destruction of the Spanish fleet in Manila Bay, which made Commodore Dewey one of the most lionized heroes in our history. In a frenzy of enthusiasm Congress made him an admiral and for good measure stipulated that he could never be retired. For some days before the news of the battle "broke" I heard my Father and the neighbors discuss what might be the meaning of the ominous silence surrounding the maneuvers of Dewey's squadron. Had it been sunk? The mystery was cleared up when it was learned that prior to the battle, Dewey had ordered the cable to be cut. For some years I had in my possession a souvenir of Dewey's achievement, which I bought in Moline and wore on the lapel of my coat. It was a metallic American flag, with a pendant in the form of a cartridge. The display card read as follows: "Old Glory and Dewey's Pills for Spaniards."

News of the other major defeat for the Spanish navy thrilled me in the early days of July. Within less than two weeks after the battle of Santiago Bay, the land forces defending Santiago de Cuba surrendered on July 16th. The same issue of the Rock Island newspaper that carried the news of the surrender published the obituary of my Father, who passed away in his sixty-fourth year at the hour the whistles were blowing to celebrate the victory on land that virtually put an end to enemy resistance in Cuba.

During the sixteen weeks of war the newspapers and illustrated weeklies and monthlies spread a feast before their readers. I read about cities and countries that had no meaning until I looked them up on the map. It wasn't until after the elapse of two or more years that the details of the scandals of the war were exposed before a disillusioned public. Only the exceptional paper opposed the declaration of war; and during hostilities the public was not told about the inefficiency and corruption in the conduct of the war.

Even my hero of the Battle of Santiago Bay, Commodore Schley, was impelled to ask for a court of inquiry to investigate his conduct during the war. The court of inquiry with Admiral Dewey dissenting rendered a report in general adverse to Schley. Moreover, it was disheartening to a boy of high school age, who had read about the "cruel and treacherous" Spaniards, to learn of the jealousy and inefficiency of our officers, the poor condition of some of the "crack" ships of our navy, and the emaciated condition of returning soldiers who did not conceal their contempt for the commissary and for contractors who furnished food unfit for consumption and shoddy uniforms and inferior equipment.

The-presidential campaign of 1900 was waged when the American people were vexed over the problems, which the war had saddled on their country. The words "imperialism" and "militarism" were brought into the political forum. Both major parties harbored imperialists and anti-imperialists. The Republicans renominated

McKinley. The Democrats renominated Bryan on a platform denouncing imperialism and militarism, which Bryan featured as the "paramount" issue. My political views were not mature enough to count in the ballot box; but if I had been of voting age there would have been one more vote for McKinley and Roosevelt. Nothing had happened between 1896 and 1900 to weaken my allegiance to the political orthodoxy of my family. I heard Bryan speak, but his eloquence made no greater appeal than it made in the previous campaign.

VIII
HIGHER EDUCATION

A great teacher forms the minds of his students unconsciously, just as great literature forms the mind and molds character.

My education from the academy through the graduate school was acquired in the last years of the nineteenth century and the first years of the twentieth century. The idealism and optimism of the American people were in full bloom. Prosperity, industry, and thrift were reflected in homes, schools and colleges, libraries, churches, newspapers, periodicals, philanthropic foundations, legislation, recreation, and the general welfare. Apostles of social justice, political integrity, and peace and good will toward men were given respectful hearing in the pulpit, on the platform, and on the printed page. Self-seekers who would blight the fine traditions and culture bequeathed by the Puritan founding fathers were excoriated in the pages of popular magazines and newspapers.

It was a good time to be on a campus of a college and a university—good for members of the faculty as well for students. Salaries and incomes were small by contrast with a later generation, but so were living costs for faculty families and for students. It is not far from the truth to say that an education was within reach of adolescents who wanted and deserved an education.

The educational institution in which I enrolled after finishing the grades was a combined theological seminary, college, academy, business college, and conservatory of music. The campus population of Augustana College and Theological Seminary was <u>sui generis</u> to Swedish America. It was recruited in rural and urban communities from the Atlantic Coast to the Rocky Mountains. Farmers, miners, sailors, and common laborers predominated. These young men—some of' them weren't so young—burned midnight oil over Caesar's Gallic War and Xenophon's Anabasis to prepare for the high calling of ministering to their fellow countrymen. Literary societies, debating clubs, oratorical contests, missionary societies, prayer meetings, the Handel Oratorio Society, the band, and the orchestra took precedence over non-existent dances, bridge parties, fraternities, week-end parties, and football games.

The organization of the institution conformed to the pattern of the other educational institutions of the church which supported them. Meager financial resources burdened the faculty with heavy teaching loads. The inadequate and understaffed library was housed on the third floor of the main building. The laboratory equipment was pathetic. A distinguished scientist, whose research in the field of geology brought scholars from institutions as remote as Harvard to consult him, taught English in the second class of the academy four days a week from four to five o'clock. I was a member of that class. I did not know that the constitution of the State of Illinois prohibited cruel and unusual punishments.

College Faculties and the Quality of Teaching

Members of the faculty taught classes in both academy and college and even in the theological seminary. Students were allowed to carry unreasonably heavy programs. Obviously, all too many students were hustled into the theological seminary without adequate training in college and academy. It was not unusual for a student to pursue studies in the academy and college simultaneously. Even men in the college were taking work in the seminary.

Before I walked the campus as a student, I was on speaking terms with members of the faculty and many students. My home in Iowa was a sort of clearinghouse for preachers, students, and immigrants; and after we moved to Rock Island students and professors and clergymen borrowed dabs of money from my father.

It was an invaluable experience to be a part of the process of Americanization, to see with one's own eyes the "American transition," even if few, perhaps none of us, were aware of the role we were playing in an interesting chapter of history. The "Common Man's Utopia" was too obvious to be understood and written about objectively.

Few of the members of the historical profession had the language equipment to write the history of immigration; and there had been no systematic effort to collect the necessary documents. Historians had not directed attention to the human map in order to explain how the fabric of American society was woven.

It goes without saying that the "green Swedes" from the "Swede college" provoked mirth, ridicule, and disdain from citizens of Rock Island and Moline. Some thirty years after I had left the halls of the college, I had the privilege of attending the dedicatory exercises of the Wallberg Hall of Science, when I met Augustana's most distinguished alumnus whom I had not seen for more than a score of years. He surprised me by inquiring if I was a son of the retired Iowa farmer who lived near the campus. "You were just a little kid then," he said, and then he added: "Had you ever before, and have you ever since, seen anything as green as I was in those days?"

The distinguished scientist, in a formal address at the dedicatory exercises, paid a tribute to the late professor of natural science who, he said, had little more than a ball of string and a table to work with. "What you need here is men," he stated, "and the buildings will take care of themselves."

The faculty did the best it could with the miscellaneous student body. Burdened with a heavy teaching load containing a variety of subjects, they had no course other than to resort to the use of textbooks. Notwithstanding, through the years I have cherished the memory of professors whose personality and character obscured their pedagogy.

What makes a good teacher? What do students carry away from the classroom of the great teacher? My favorite teacher at Augustana was one of the poorest pedagogues among the teachers I have had as an undergraduate and graduate student. For earnest and intellectually alert students he was a good teacher in spite of his methodology, which seems to prove that students who are in college to educate themselves are the only ones who get a real education.

The test of an education is not the amount of knowledge that a student accumulates. If he leaves the campus with an appetite to know, instead of with a mind like a cistern into which has been poured undigested information, he will have a taste for knowledge and the capacity to assimilate it. A great teacher forms the minds of his students unconsciously, just as great literature forms the mind and molds character. According to a law of delayed action, teachers do not see the most important results in their students. It is only in later years that students appreciate the seeds that the great teacher sows on the fertile mind. Maturity and experience give life and meaning to ideas that have lain dormant.

Samuel Johnson said that there is as much difference between a lettered and an unlettered man as there is between the living and the dead. The man whose mind is stored with germinal passages found in great literature is a new creation. In the words of St. Paul, to be filled with the Spirit is "speaking to yourselves in psalms and hymns and spiritual songs, singing and making melody in your heart to the Lord." In the classroom of a great teacher are stored up knowledge and spiritual truth whose real meaning may be revealed in later years.

Augustana College furnished opportunities for self-education, partly because there were so few sideshows to attract attention. There were lectures and concerts on the Lyceum course, and members of the faculty gave occasional lectures to societies and organizations to promote interest in various fields of knowledge. There were no pressure groups, no socialist or communist clubs, not even a Republican organization. The voices of propagandists and "do-gooders" were silent. Debating societies discussed issues of the day; literary societies sponsored programs of declamations, talks, and essays; there were societies of belles letters; there were musical organizations. We heard little or nothing about racial or religious intolerance. There was no discrimination based on social distinction or membership in fraternities or sororities.

The professor of history taught history according to old-fashioned methods. In every course he used an outline, which he wrote on the blackboard as he lectured informally. The examinations were based exclusively on the outlines, with emphasis on chronology. In spite of the teacher's limitations, his classes were interesting, and there was dignity in his treatment of the subject. There was no frivolity or cheap humor in his classes.

The greatest scholar on the faculty was the professor of natural science who taught botany and zoology in the academy and meteorology, geology, physiology, and structural botany in the college. I enjoyed most the course in geology, partly because that was his special field and partly because as a senior I had a better appreciation of scholarship. Modest man that he was, I do not recall that he ever mentioned to his classes anything he had written. On geological and botanical excursions he was in his element doing research. I think I profited most by observing his methods through which he unconsciously revealed his scholarly instincts.

The professor of English also taught philosophy, ethics, sociology, and logic. In the conservatory of music he taught psychology in relation to music and used his own textbook. His courses in literature were hit or miss and were weak on background. There was almost no interpretation of the period in which the author wrote. For all we knew, Shakespeare or Milton might have produced their masterpieces in the fifteenth or the eighteenth century. We learned next to nothing about the personality and the career of the author.

On the other side of this picture, the professor's instincts were excellent. He knew good and wholesome literature. I do not recollect reading anything cheap or shoddy. Unlike some teachers of literature, he did not ask students to read something just because it was in print or because he had done research on an author, however obscure or third rate. I learned from this teacher that the best service a teacher of literature can render is to expose his students to authors whose works have stood the test of time -- in other words, to let the masterpieces work their miracles in heart and soul and to make the teacher's lectures secondary. This professor was a good teacher in spite of his methodology.

Judged by pedagogical standards, the best teacher I have ever had was the man who taught Latin in the academy and German in the college. He was unmerciful. You had to know every declension, conjugation, irregular verb, every rule governing articles, prepositions, and cases. I learned the grammar by heart from the first page to the last. My chief criticism of the professor's college teaching is that he was content to hear the students translate, decline, conjugate, parse, and analyze, without presenting some interpretation of the author. He was a drillmaster, not a lecturer. This shortcoming was overbalanced by his sterling qualities and character. There was no sham or pretense in his makeup, no concessions to popularity or public relations. His ruthless thoroughness was the expression of flair for accuracy and system and abhorrence for students whose ambition was to "get by". Only in later years long after I had left the campus did I become acquainted with the other nature of the teacher whom we called the "shark in languages". He was a man of wide interests and kindly nature.

The Good and the Bad in Literature

When I was an undergraduate, books were so cheap that a student of limited funds could accumulate a modest library. Never before or since have newsstands and reading rooms displayed such a large assortment of excellent magazines and periodicals at moderate prices. Monthlies and weeklies had a brilliant array of talent among authors and artists. By contrast with the periodicals published after the First World War, the enduring quality of contents of the *Century*, *Harper's*, *Scribner's*, *Atlantic Monthly*, *North American Review*, and *Review of Reviews* is impressive. Moreover, the post-war generation had nothing to compare with the half-dozen ten-cent monthlies, which enjoyed a large circulation. Parents and children of a later generation were deprived of the wholesome and dignified material in the *Outlook*, the *Independent*, *Harper's Weekly*, the *Youth's Companion*, and *Harper's Young People*.

The present generation has forgotten, if it ever knew, that there is no worse robber than a bad book and a bad magazine. During my undergraduate years I read much more of my own choice than I read in connection with formal courses. Publishers like the A. L. Burt Company, Rand McNally and Company, and Grosset and Dunlap printed volumes of standard fiction priced at twenty-five cents. The authors included Dickens, Thackeray, Kingsley, Bulwer Lytton, George Eliot, Miss Mulock, Kipling, Scott, Read, Irving, and Hawthorne. There were popular priced works by Addison, Macaulay, Carlyle, Lamb, Lowell, Longfellow, Emerson, and Tennyson.

It was not until I was in my senior year at the University of Chicago that I made the acquaintance of authors whose books would have been rejected by a nineteenth century American publisher as obscene and beyond the limits of decency. The two courses were listed, respectively, as "English Literature, 1660-1700" and "English Literature, 1744-4798." I have my lecture motes before me. In the notebook for the later course I read: "The novels are not virginibus puerisque. They dwell on the seamy side of life. The animal in men receives too much attention. The incidents and language and sometimes the plot are vulgar. But these novels are shocking rather than corrupting."

The professor who conducted the other course announced that he could not conscientiously require us to read the Restoration Comedy, which included such writers as Wycherley, Congreve, Vanbrugh, and Farquhar. In the lecture notes for that course I find the following notations: "Some hold that literature has the privilege of representing anything pertaining to life. Some artists say that if they can present any character whatsoever in an artistic manner, there is nothing to be said against it. In presenting evil for the purposes of rebuke, there is danger that rebuke wears off and temptation and curiosity remain. The Comedy of the Restoration corrupted morals of the people and made the condition of society worse in a degree. Shakespeare took deliberate delight in dealing with dirty things, but they fade into insignificance because he is such a large mind."

Someone has said that metaphysics is "the giving of bad reasons for what we believe on instinct." As an undergraduate I was only remotely exposed to metaphysics, and I didn't even hear of psychoanalysis. I do not find the term in the index of William James's *Psychology* (copyright, 1892), which was the textbook used in the course I took. A distinguished scholar remarked to me some years ago that we will never know what modern psychology has done to us. I suppose he had in mind psychoanalysis, which has displaced what the nineteenth century called morality.

W. R. Inge, misnamed the "gloomy dean," had no doubt that the Elizabethan and the Victorian ages would appear to the historian of the near future as the twin peaks in which English civilization culminated. He said that England would be wise to stick to its great tradition in fiction instead of preferring the corrupt following of the French. He was convinced that the palmiest days of English novel writing were in the middle of the nineteenth century, when Dickens, Thackeray, Charlotte Bronte, George Eliot, Anthony Trollope, Kingsley, Disraeli, Bulwer Lytton, and Meredith were all writing. He also considered the wonderful variety of strong and beautiful prose, which that age, produced. Froude, Macaulay, Newman, Ruskin, Pater, and Stevenson are each supreme in very different styles; and all of them achieved excellence by an amount of labor which very few writers are now willing to bestow.

Tennyson, he said, wrote beautifully about beautiful things, including beautiful conduct. He saw that the Victorian social order was breaking up, and foretold many of the evils that have since come upon us. Inge stated that even in fiction the note of disillusionment was heard with increasing clearness. Addressing himself to younger readers in 1922, the dean would not prophesy what England would be like thirty years hence. "We old Victorians will before then have made room for you by quitting a world to which, I am sure you think, we no longer belong."

During my undergraduate years I was blissfully ignorant of the existence of the prophet of doom. It was not until the catastrophe of the First World War that I learned to know the world we lived in. Even so, the magnitude of the crisis was not revealed until after the Second World War, when the issue was distinctly drawn between brute force and the Christian faith, which is the greatest of all idealisms.

It was not until after the First World War that I read Max Nordau's *Degeneration* and an article in the *Quarterly Review* for February 1894, which was inspired by that book. The article was entitled "Is Europe Going Mad? A Study of Modern Literature". Nordau was a Positivist who denied God, the soul, and the judgment to come, and regarded the individual as but an unimportant episode in the life of all. He approached Modern European literature from the standpoint of the student of mental pathology. The characteristic~ of modern fashion, he found, is a diseased imitation of other periods, a singularity which is never original. He discovered tokens of confusion in dress, decoration, and manners. Bishop Butler asked whether nations could go mad. Nordau replied in the affirmative. He believed that the evidence of the hysteria of the masses was found in statistics of crime, insanity, and suicide. The present race of Europeans has weakened their nerve centers by the use of narcotics and artificial excitement.

Nordau was not without hostile critics who challenged his observations and conclusions; but there were also contemporaries who believed that the great day of visitation for Europe was drawing nigh. Some of them found at the bottom of the social disturbance the dissolution of fundamental beliefs and the revolt of women.

Some years before the publication of Nordau's book, Matthew Arnold foretold the downfall of France. He found the symptoms of the disease that was eating away the vigor of the people in the character of the popular novels, plays, and periodicals. He saw that the press, drama, and fiction provoked artificial lustfulness. In France, as in other countries, it was the minority that had set the standard by its moral and mental stability. In other words, a wholesome public opinion was maintained by a small element of the population, which was beaten down and lost its influence.

Living in exile in Italy in the latter years of the nineteenth century, Louis Kossuth, one of the great heroes of the mid-century revolutions in Europe, died in 1894, a worn, weary, and disheartened old man, a Jeremiah in exile. He was certain that Europe was on the verge of a vast conflict. Society was sick of a malady that defied cure. "There seems to be no remedy," he said. "Meanwhile, the earth will continue to revolve, and some day the present population may be swept from its surface, and a new race, capable of a new civilization, may appear. A cataclysm is the only hope of solution."

IX
LIFE AS A PROFESSOR

It fell to my lot to explore three highly controversial fields: the American public domain, immigration, and religion.

I began my-college teaching of history at the University of Minnesota in a war-torn world. A few days after I had completed my graduate work, newspapers reported the assassination of the Archduke Francis Joseph, heir to the Austro-Hungarian throne, at Serajevo, Bosnia. A month later Austria declared war on Serbia, and within a few days Europe was an armed camp. On August 2, 1914, Germany declared war on Russia.

In retrospect, I have come to the reluctant conclusion that there is as much collective political wisdom to be found in conversations with the so-called man in the street as I have gathered from conversations with businessmen, clergymen, lawyers, doctors, and teachers. Lincoln placed his trust in the plain people.

Jefferson is popularly known as the great exponent of democracy and equality; but his proposed plan of education was rigidly selective. He believed that there was a natural aristocracy among men, based on virtue and talents. The natural aristocracy he considered as the precious gift of nature for the instruction, the trusts, and the government of society. Jefferson always had in view the objective of making good citizens. He put in a plug for history by stating that by apprizing citizens of the past it would enable them to judge of the future by availing them of the experience of other times and nations. It would enable them to know ambition under every guise, which it might assume.

A century and a half after Jefferson's optimistic appraisal of the value of the study of history, a distinguished president of a distinguished American university in a public address developed the thesis that the study of American history is the best defense against propaganda. If the president had been a historian instead of a scientist, he would have known that every age writes its own history and that the appraisal of textbooks in history by school boards and by committees of Congress is as subjective as is their approval or disapproval of candidates for public office. A textbook that attracts large adoptions in New England may find little favor in other sections.

Historical subjects are more or less controversial. It fell to my lot to explore three highly controversial fields: the American public domain, immigration, and religion. These subjects are the warp and woof of American history.

A Professional Choice: The History of Immigration

It was my good fortune to write my doctor's thesis on the *Political History of the Public Lands from 1840 to 1862* under the direction of Professor Frederick Jackson Turner who became a member of the Harvard faculty in 1910, after having resigned his professorship in the University of Wisconsin.

In his paper on "The Significance of the Frontier in American History" and in almost every product of his pen he discoursed on the "peculiar importance of American history for understanding the processes of social development." He never swerved from the conviction that "free lands in the United States have been the most important single factor in explaining our development." He told me that early in life it was his intention to make the public lands a life study.

Professor Turner was essentially an explorer—always raising questions and always interested in trends, processes, and developments. He would marshal a formidable army of facts, but only for the purpose of presenting points of view. He was not primarily interested in establishing the time and place of the birth of the first white child west of the Mississippi River. He cautioned me against becoming too excited over a phase of history. "Read around it," he said.

I could not have chosen a better subject than the public lands to elucidate Turner's dictum that the "frontier and the section are two of the most fundamental factors in American history." Legislation and proposed legislation with reference to the disposal and administration of the public lands was favored or opposed according to the advantages it gave to a section or to a special interest. Perhaps the most powerful single vested interest in opposition to liberal land legislation was the institution of slavery, which was localized in a section whose leaders felt that it was falling behind the other sections. The homestead bill was regarded as a scheme to settle the Northwest and to create new states where the settlers would be free-soilers, that is, opposed to the extension of the institution of slavery.

The debate on the homestead bill in Congress and in the newspapers instructed me in the principles and doctrine of nativism. Before the Civil War, native as well as foreign-born citizens of the United States who expressed anti-slavery sentiments were charged by the defenders of the institution of slavery as harboring un-American sentiments. They were accused of attacking an established institution because slavery was established by state laws and was recognized in the federal Constitution. The abolitionists countered by stating that an evil does not lose its deformity by becoming an institution. On the contrary, an evil entrenched behind institutions was on that very account to be assailed with all the weapons of reason, of moral suasion, and of moral reprobation.

Certain questions have recurred in every generation: Is conscience to stoop from its supremacy and become the echo of the human magistrate? Is humanity a local feeling? Does sympathy stop at a frontier? Can people screen themselves behind nationality or race or church from the moral judgment of the world? Is there room in America for a church or a sect or a national group or any organization that would impose a mental quarantine?

These are dangerous questions to raise in any country in any age. Attempts to answer them have sent individuals to the gallows and to jails and have plunged nations and continents into war and tumult. These and similar questions are in the background and sometimes in the foreground when men set themselves to the task of devising instruments of government, of adjusting relations between minorities and majorities, of promoting the public welfare, and of securing the blessings of liberty.

Partly as the result of my research on the public lands and partly as the result of my heritage, I became interested in the history of immigration. I saw that the student of American history had a large task ahead of him to explain how the human map of America was drawn and to isolate the germs that made hundreds of thousands of Europeans sick of their lot. They crossed the Atlantic for their spiritual, economic, social, and political health. It is significant that in the nineteenth century histories of individual immigrants stocks were usually written in a foreign language. The older general works on immigration were based largely on statistics and official documents and seemed to lose sight of the fact that the emigrant and the immigrant were the same person.

The old immigrant groups continued their native languages as spoken languages into the twentieth century. They were free to work out their own religious, economic, and social salvation. They established their own newspapers, churches, schools, academies, colleges, theological seminaries, and societies. These groups and their cultures were sometimes singled out by scholars and by crusaders as obstacles to the wholesome development of American institutions.

X
DISCOVERING SWEDISH ROOTS

I left Sweden with enhanced appreciation for and better understanding of my own country, as well as for the land from which my parents emigrated.

My intensive research in the field of immigration was applied to Sweden, where it was my privilege to spend a year on a stipend from the John Simon Guggenheim Memorial Foundation.

Our family arrived in Stockholm on September 20, 1927, and within a few days I was in quest of the answer to the question why hundreds of thousands of men and women deserted the Land of the Midnight Sun in favor of the great republic across the Atlantic. What forces conspired to produce the exodus that caused alarm lest the country be depopulated? Superficially, the answer is simple as I learned almost as soon as I set my foot on Swedish soil; and after a sojourn of a few weeks, I was tempted to conclude that my research could take the form of cousin hunting in the cottages of Sweden.

Finding America in Sweden

In homes from the southern tip of the peninsula to the snowy peaks of the north, I found pictures of the Minneapolis Courthouse, the Woolworth Building in New York, and Chicago's skyscrapers. After the inevitable cups of coffee, mothers proudly brought photographs of Carl, August, Sven, Helga, Inga, and Stina. Helga was employed in Minneapolis until she married and settled on a large farm thickly populated with chickens and livestock and served by an automobile. Carl is the mayor of a town in Minnesota; Sven is the foreman of a furniture factory in Rockford, Illinois; Stina sends us money from the profits of her dress shop in Jamestown, New York. "You say you live in Minneapolis. August lives in Seattle. Be sure to tell him that you saw us." And so it went as we moved from home to home. The rector of a parish in southern Sweden who responded favorably to my telephone request to examine the parish records in his custody surprised me at his doorstep by expressing pleasure at meeting a former fellow townsman. He explained in good English that for some years he had officiated as rector in Swedish Episcopal churches in Minneapolis and St. Paul.

The greatest surprise of all awaited me in the province of Småland, the spawning ground of whole schools of emigrants who found their way through the waves of the Atlantic to the ten thousand lakes of Minnesota. While the conversation passed over the coffee cups in the home of a prosperous farmer, I was informed that he had in his possession a letter that might be of interest to me. It proved to be a letter dated at Jefferson County, Iowa, in 1854, and signed by my grandfather. It was a long narrative about his own experiences and about the fortunes of members of his family since the time of their emigration in 1849. "Would you like to have that letter?" inquired my host. He was not in the tourist business, and all he asked was a promise to send him a typed copy of the letter after my return to the United States.

There was zest in running down literally scores of cousins and near-cousins in an automobile. The clues that revealed the location of their homes were found in the parish records deposited in provincial archives, in parsonages, and in churches. In these documents I found notations like the following: "Immigrated to America," "Absconded to America," "Said to have gone to America." The "open sesame" to almost every home was a personal reference to a member of the family who had fallen victim to "America fever."

I represented myself as a descendant of immigrants who was interested in meeting friends and relatives of immigrants of whom I made mention. I made no mention of my profession. It was fortunate that I took this precaution. The rural folk stood in such awe of the much-abused title "professor" in America that I became convinced that it <u>was</u> a distinction. In my own country I shared the title with high divers, sleight-of hand performers, and patent medicine vendors. In one of' the first parishes we visited a thrifty housewife confided to my wife, after she had inquired about my vocation, that if she and her husband had known beforehand that I was a professor, they would not have opened their home to us. She added, however, that they had no regrets, because they had learned that we were "nice people anyway."

During ten months of research I accumulated a vast amount of material extracted from manuscripts, newspapers, official documents, and a wide variety of other material. These sources took on new meaning as the result of conversations in the cottages from which men and women in their best years bade farewell to parents and sisters and brothers.

The magic that transformed these humble folk into Americans can best be detected in letters written by immigrants to friends and relatives left behind. These so-called "America letters" expressed remarkable satisfaction with the new country, and revealed that the writers were Americans in spirit even before they embarked on the greatest adventure of their lives. The contents of these letters from another world were so fabulous that editors of newspapers published them and thereby infected parish after parish with "America fever."

These letters were read aloud in homes, at markets and fairs, and in crowds assembled at parish churches. Social, religious, political, and economic institutions in America worked like an elixir on the writers; and their enthusiasm betrayed them into exaggeration. They became evangelists preaching the gospel of America to the heavy-laden. For them the year of jubilee had come.

My observations and research in Sweden convinced

me that one of the striking contrasts between the United States and Europe lies in the field of religion. In the United States religion became laicized – democratized. The established churches in Europe were fortresses of sacerdotalism. Clericalism was quick to suppress conventicals as dangerous to "pure doctrine" and as threats to the prerogatives of the clerical estate, whereas in America there was room for Christians who questioned the validity of ecclesiastical regulations and legislative enactments which denied the right of a man to teach publicly in church and to administer the sacraments, unless he was ordained and set apart in the clerical estate.

The historian Lecky wrote that the chief triumph of a religious movement is not to be found in its action upon large classes of the community, or within the noisy arena of politics. It is to be found rather in those spheres and movements of life that beyond all others are secluded from the eye of history.

The leaders of religious reform in Sweden were in many cases men of simple faith and of humble birth, who were unskilled in statesmanship and untutored in ecclesiastical polity. Some of them were returned emigrants who had drunk deeply of American idealism. Baptist and Methodist pioneers in Sweden had been schooled in the methods employed by leaders in the New World. Temperance crusaders had read sermons, tracts, and books prepared by reformers in the United States. One of the most influential crusaders was an English Methodist, George Scott, who in 1841 visited the United States to solicit funds for the erection of a chapel in Stockholm and for the prosecution of his campaign in the provinces.

Among the immigrant stocks, none have assimilated more rapidly than have the Swedes. They have shown feeble resistance to Americanization, because they brought with them from the Old Country a minimum amount of baggage that might have impeded the process. Moreover, they were closely related in race, religion, and history with the old American stock; and they were fortunate in the time of their arrival when the vast spaces of the Mississippi Valley were opening for settlement. In this region of free and cheap land, of unlimited opportunities, and of unbounded optimism, they found nothing that seriously challenged their way of life. Except for an occasional discordant voice, their leaders expressed remarkable satisfaction with their adopted country. The clergy had been emancipated from a moribund established church, and the laity had been freed from the shackles of a stratified society.

I began my study of Swedish immigration at about the time the Congress of the United States enacted the most drastic immigration bill ever to be approved by the president of the United States down to that time. This was in 1924. Simultaneously, Sweden abandoned her anti-emigration propaganda, which got under way in the first decade of the twentieth century. The rising tide of sentiment against emigration was one expression of a national renaissance. Books, pamphlets, and editorials were designed to stimulate patriotism and a sense of responsibility for the defense of the fatherland. A program to make the country a more desirable place to live was inaugurated. It was also proposed to enact a law to prohibit the emigration of men eligible for military service. In Sweden, as in other countries in Europe, the United States was "the country without compulsory military service." In Sweden it was not so much that the average young man was unwilling to serve his country—he rebelled against the haughty and starchy military caste. Moreover, an important element among the free-church people objected to the immoral atmosphere of camp life. Although there was objection to compulsory military service because it was contrary to freedom of conscience, the chief objection was that it exposed young men to vice, gambling, and the oaths of officers.

The fundamental cause of the collapse of the anti-emigration campaign is to be found in the genius and traditions of the Swedish people. Any legislation or proposed legislation that ran counter to their conception of freedom of conscience and of the freedom of the individual was doomed to failure. Sweden is intensely protestant, and her sons and daughters in the American republic are as zealous defenders of freedom of conscience and of the right of private judgment as are the descendants of the Pilgrims and the Puritans.

In 1883, when emigration was at high tide, a Stockholm journalist in reporting his observations in Swedish settlements in the United States suggested that the way to stop emigration was "to move America over to Sweden." His magic formula was to increase opportunities for employment, to respect the workingmen, to assist him to become a freeholder, and to remove restrictions on religious freedom -- in short, to make Sweden a better country. The world knows about the "Middle Way."

I left Sweden with enhanced appreciation for and better understanding of my own country, as well as for the land from which my parents emigrated. I was conscious of living in a foreign country; but from the beginning I sensed that I was in a friendly country. My wife, whose parents emigrated from Sweden, had the same experience. Our sons, George and Gordon, whose ages were eight and six, were excellent barometers. After what appeared to be a slow start in learning to speak Swedish, within two or three months they were speaking Swedish to each other at play; and it wasn't many weeks before they were correcting our pronunciation of certain difficult words—difficult for persons who spoke peasant Swedish. Incidentally, as we grew better acquainted, some of our friends informed me that I spoke the dialect of Småland, the province where my parents were born.

More than once our sons returned from shopping in the neighborhood proudly to announce that proprietors or clerks had pointed them out to their customers with comments that only a few weeks earlier they were unable to speak a word of Swedish. Even before Christmas, their assimilation had reached the stage where they cautioned their parents against speaking English on the street for fear of being taken for "foreigners." That friendly warning was enlightening in view of the post-war drive to forbid the teaching of foreign languages in the American schools, and the accompanying Americanization movement.

Becoming American: The Inevitable Assimilation

At the time of our stay in Sweden there was an organization bearing the name Society for the Preservation of Swedish Culture in Foreign Lands. Notwithstanding the zeal of the group interested in the work of the society, responsible citizens accepted the assimilation of the Swedes in the United States as inevitable and desirable. They either took no interest in the campaign to preserve Swedish as a spoken language, or else saw the futility of it.

In an interview published in a Stockholm daily, Nyheter, February 28,1928, I stated that it was impossible to prevent the inevitable. If Sweden and the United States ever establish a cultural entente cordiale, it will not be a hothouse product of propaganda, but the fruit of a slow, gradual process. With the extinction of Swedish as a spoken language, Swedish may be cultivated by the few who have the inclination and the ability. When that day dawns, I continued, the transatlantic pilgrims will visit libraries, art galleries, and ancient churches, instead of gazing upon the old homestead and inquiring as to the whereabouts of confirmation mates.

I explained that the immigrants found America a paradise in contrast with the Old Country. The second generation learned to speak Swedish in the home and to know Sweden as a land of poverty and class distinctions. On the school grounds the children of immigrants were ashamed of their foreign language, not because it was

Swedish but because it set them apart from the "American children." In the third generation Swedish as a spoken language has all but disappeared.

In the years that have passed since our visit to Sweden, the relations between the people of Swedish blood on both sides of the Atlantic have become increasingly cordial and understanding. With the steady retreat of the Swedish language—turned into a rout by the First World War—churches of Swedish origin have lost their membership based exclusively on language and background. Distinguished Swedish scholars have served as visiting professors in American universities and colleges and have returned to their own institutions with pleasant memories of American hospitality and respect for American educational institutions -- faculties, libraries, laboratories, and classroom facilities. And American scholars have profited by associations established at Uppsala, Lund, and Stockholm.

The assimilation of an immigrant stock has been retarded in proportion to the efforts of leaders to transplant the feudalities and usages of Europe. Whether in the religious or in the secular sphere, the Swedish immigrants have not been shackled by excessive institutionalism or hampered by frustrations or enmities ingrained in Europe. In the United States they were emancipated from traditions and mores, which fostered corporate pride. Pressure groups were few and ineffective.

Very little inspiration to preserve their language and culture came from Sweden. The idea of building up a Swedish nationality in the United States was repugnant and chimerical. Every friend of the United States, it was stated, ought to wish that all nationalities might be fused there. Certainly nothing should be done to hinder fusion. What would be the reaction in Sweden, it was asked, if Germans, Finns, and Russians should encourage immigration to Sweden in order to strengthen their own nationalities?

In the earliest years of the immigration movement

there were abortive efforts in a few settlements to establish Swedish parochial schools. The Swedish immigrants had no fear of the public schools. Indeed, these were looked upon as one of the great advantages America offered. Parents were proud of their "American" children and rejoiced in their progress in school.

In common with other immigrant stocks, the first and second generation Swedes organized Swedish-American societies and clubs. The fact that these organizations had greater attractions for individuals without church affiliations would indicate that in common with most institutional churches the Swedish American churches had at least four compartments: (1) social; (2) educational; (3) eleemosynary; and (4) religious. They are not watertight compartments, nor are they mutually exclusive. There are members who belong in all four. The immigrants who were religiously inclined naturally affiliated with congregations where they could have fellowship with kindred souls who spoke the language of their youth. Notwithstanding, these organizations, religious and secular, recruited few members relative to the total population.

A Wholly American Perspective

During the first year of the Second World War, I had the pleasure of conferring with a man who was doing special work for the Coordinator of Information. He had traveled extensively in the United States and in Europe and was well informed about "foreign" settlements in this country. His conversations with people of Swedish birth and descent in the United States convinced him that their attitude toward the war before and after Pearl Harbor was not in the least influenced by Sweden's fortunes.